Europe is in my DNA

First Published 2021

Printed By:-
www.lulu.com

ISBN 978 1 716 26119 0

Introduction

This blog covers the period 15th April 2018 to 18th April 2019.

On the 23rd March 2019 I went on my first (and probably last) political march to stop Brexit. It was fun, glad I did it but as I knew at the time, utterly pointless. All the Brexit nonsense of this period seems so irrelevant now that we are in lockdown. This is because the Government now have the convenient excuse that Coronavirus is the cause of any economic issues we have in the future.

My Nephew was the next person to do a DNA test so there are confirmations of the Brain tree but unfortunately no confirmations of the Brain or Swan lines as yet. Then my Mum did a test at Christmas. This resulted in so many Barber matches, currently 176. Her test was very handy as it confirmed many lines, especially the Green one.

The best DNA matches were the ones that confirmed Alexander Mustart. This meant that I finally had some Paterson cousins to write about. I did not match any, the DNA skipped me and went straight to my children and nephew.

On a personal perspective I did my first (and only) 10k. We went to Liverpool and did the whole Beatles thing. Then we got a Cocker Spaniel/English Bulldog cross called Betty. Football fever hit the country in July as England were doing well in the World Cup but lost against Croatia in the semifinals. It was another hottest summer on record. Of course the weather broke just before our caravan holiday in Cornwall at the end of August. I went to Beckenham Crematorium to meet up with my 2nd cousin as he was moving to Belgium because of Brexit. This was so he could show me the location of our 2nd Great Grandfathers grave before he left. We also had another city break, this time to Paris. We was at Notre Dame a month before it caught on fire.

Sarah Ashley

19th April 2020

Part One

1.   posted 15 Apr 2018, 16:58

Have done the first book, decided for ease and speed not to include any pictures.   However, I still made a mistake.   The project is called 'geneology' not 'genealogy'.

Book 3

2.   posted 19 Apr 2018, 16:24

'DNA Ramblings of an Amateur Genealogist Part One' has arrived! It looks okay considering the speedy way in which I compiled it.

On Tuesday I pretty much spent all day on Part Two. I have formatted it, so it is the same as books 1 and 2 which I didn't do for book 3. I still haven't finished it though because I really want to include some photos and tree pictures. I cannot seem to get them looking nice at all.

Part 2

3.   posted 19 Apr 2018, 22:19

I got the trees in. I think the page numbers are weird so handy I don't have a contents page. Anyway, very bored of getting it to look nice now so have just ordered it.

Book 4

4.   posted 26 Apr 2018, 14:47

Part Two has arrived and the page numbers are up the spout. Go to 12. Then start again to 4 with some blanks. Then they start for a final time but just on the even side! Ah well, not important. The trees and pictures look good which is important.

I think daughter said she wants to take this one to school as it has the Cadbury pic in it.

Good-Bye
5.   posted 26 Apr 2018, 16:09

So the BBC has got Suits spoilers on its website, or at least *'Meghan Markle's Suits Exit Revealed'* and *'Five Moments from Meghan's last Suits'*.

Nobody has been watching it for 7 years like me. Anyone would think she is marrying a Prince in a couple of weeks' time.

I am just about to watch Season 7, Episode 16...

Thomas Barber
6.   posted 3 May 2018, 18:26

One of my Green cousins has given me a hint. I never had the wife's name for Thomas Barber. I did have it as Sarah but with no documentation to back it up. A Thomas Barber married a Keziah Arnold in 1818 but I obviously wasn't convinced that was her name as I didn't use it. My cousin says that her name is actually Sarah Hoad and this ties in with the public trees. I am going to investigate Sarah Hoad.

Onion Pie Murder
7.   posted 3 May 2018, 19:32

The real reason for the hint was to draw my attention to this: -

https://en.wikipedia.org/wiki/Onion_Pie_Murder

http://www.sussexopc.org/ParishDetails/EastSussex/Chiddingly/ChiddinglyMurder/ChiddinglyMurderB.htm

At present, I can only find a non blood link to this woman but apparently we have a blood link too: -

Sarah Ann Piper (- 1852)
wife of uncle of wife of 4th great-uncle
William French (1810 - 1852)
husband of Sarah Ann Piper
William French
father of William French
John French (1810 -)
son of William French
Sarah French (1832 - 1875)
daughter of John French
David Barber (1833 - 1912)
husband of Sarah French
Thomas Barber (1793 - 1862)
father of David Barber
Eleanor Barber (1825 - 1867)
daughter of Thomas Barber
Mercy Carley (1854 - 1909)
daughter of Eleanor Barber
Mark Green (1875 - 1935)
son of Mercy Carley

Millennium File
8. posted 3 May 2018, 19:52

The reason I didn't go with Sarah Hoad previously is because it is based on a 'Millennium File' rather than any proper document. I am sure it is correct, but I don't like accepting the Mormon related hints.

Hoad
9. posted 3 May 2018, 21:02

Few extended lines based on the wife of Thomas Barber being Sarah Hoad:-

Thomas Manser (1665 -)
8th great-grandfather
Edward Manser (1708 -)
son of Thomas Manser
Susannah Manser (1738 - 1787)
daughter of Edward Manser
Thomas Hoad (1772 - 1838)
son of Susannah Manser
Sarah Hoad (1798 - 1838)
daughter of Thomas Hoad
Eleanor Barber (1825 - 1867)
daughter of Sarah Hoad

Benjamin Clapson (1671 -)
8th great-grandfather
Mary Clapson (1708 -)
daughter of Benjamin Clapson
John Hoad (1735 - 1824)
son of Mary Clapson
Thomas Hoad (1772 - 1838)
son of John Hoad

Mary Gascain (1680 - 1747)
8th great-grandmother
Mary Clapson (1708 -)
daughter of Mary Gascain

Thomas Hoad
10. posted 4 May 2018, 09:26

I doubt there will be many Hoad stories as they all appear to be ag labs.

Anyway - a possible cousin marrying here or maybe just a surname coincidence. Can't tie it together at the moment.

Thomas Hoad is the son of Thomas Hoad and Sarah Gasson. He was born in Heathfield, Sussex on the 8th February 1797 and baptised there on the 26th March. On the 22nd February 1819 he married a Hannah Hoad.

Hannah Hoad is the daughter of William Hoad and a Sarah (public trees have Sarah Honeysett - no marriage doc confirming this yet), and she was born in Herstmonceaux on the 24th December 1793 and baptised on the 9th February 1794. There are many William Hoads so no further back. However, they all do appear to have a father called John. This John Hoad would have been born c1740 and I don't have one similar in the tree already.

Alderman
11. posted 4 May 2018, 20:33

Alderman Victor Batchelor and his wife Louisa Minnie Loader had two daughters: Minnie Louisa (1911) and Elsie Clarisse (1916).

Frederick William Richard Hoad and an unknown woman, surname Cox, had two sons: Frederick Sydney (1909) and Claude Kitchener (1915).

Frederick married Minnie in 1931 and Claude married Elsie in 1938.

Local
12. posted 5 May 2018, 10:42

Thursday saw England voting in local elections. Bromley had the added twist of being a pilot for having to show ID in order to vote.

Anyway - no surprises, UKIP lost 123 seats and they were split between the other parties. Now they have caused the Brexit problem there is no need for them anymore.

Sad

13. posted 7 May 2018, 19:40

Ruth Hoad was born in Heathfield on the 28th June 1804 and was baptised there on the 29th July. On the 28th January 1832 she married Richard Hollands.

They lived in Bodiam, Sussex. Their first daughter, Hannah, was baptised on the 6th May 1833. They had another daughter, Ruth, c1835 but cannot find her baptism doc. Their first son Walter followed a few years later, baptised on the 31st July 1836. Godfrey was born c1838, cannot find a baptism doc for him either. James was baptised on the 28th April 1839, David was born c1840. In 1841, there were a family of 8. Ruth and Richard had another son, William, baptised on the 23rd May 1842. Bringing the family to 9.

Then at the end of 1843 something happened.

Hannah, aged 10, died.
Ruth, aged 8, died.
Walter, aged 7, died.
Godfrey, aged 5, died.

The family was now down to 5. I have never seen four siblings all die at the same time. Was it an illness? If so, why didn't the younger children get it? Was it a tragic accident?

Richard and Ruth went on to have two more daughters; Mary, baptised 7th January 1844 and Harriet, baptised 8th March 1846.

Ruth died in 1855 and Richard died in 1881.

Susannah
14. posted 7 May 2018, 20:50

Susannah (1794 - 1889)
mother-in-law of uncle of wife of 4th great-uncle
Sarah Ann Piper (1825 - 1852)
daughter of Susannah
William French (1821 - 1851)
husband of Sarah Ann Piper
William French
father of William French
John French (1810 -)
son of William French
Sarah French (1832 - 1875)
daughter of John French
David Barber (1833 - 1912)
husband of Sarah French
Thomas Barber (1793 - 1862)
father of David Barber
Eleanor Barber (1825 - 1867)
daughter of Thomas Barber
Mercy Carley (1854 - 1909)
daughter of Eleanor Barber
Mark Green (1875 - 1935)
son of Mercy Carley

I have searched numerous ways, but I cannot find any documentation that shows a maiden name for Susannah. If she is Hoad, she would be a bastard according to her census birth year but nothing under Gasson either.

My cousin is convinced she is Hoad though. Making her my 5th great aunt. Making the onion pie murderer my??

Susannah Hoad (1794 - 1889)
5th great-aunt
Thomas Hoad (1772 - 1838)
father of Martha Hoad
Sarah Hoad (1796 - 1838)
daughter of Thomas Hoad

Eleanor Barber (1825 - 1867)
daughter of Sarah Hoad
Mercy Carley (1854 - 1909)
daughter of Eleanor Barber
Mark Green (1875 - 1935)
son of Mercy Carley

Twelve
15. posted 7 May 2018, 21:03

My daughter is 12 tomorrow.

I really wish the relationship calculator worked like it used to. Have to
do it manually.

With no documentation such as a wedding cert for Reuben Piper or birth
docs for Susannah Hoad, the Onion Pie Murderer is:-

Sarah Ann Piper (1825 - 1852)
1st cousin 5x removed
Susannah Hoad (1794 - 1889)
mother of Sarah Ann Piper
Thomas Hoad (1772 - 1838)
father of Hannah Hoade
Sarah Hoad (1796 - 1838)
daughter of Thomas Hoad
Eleanor Barber (1825 - 1867)
daughter of Sarah Hoad
Mercy Carley (1854 - 1909)
daughter of Eleanor Barber

I don't like non confirmed. But anyway, must wrap presents.

1939
16. posted 9 May 2018, 09:19

New collection on Ancestry which could be helpful if the person is dead.
The 1939 register was actually on findmypast the other day. They have a
good explanation as to what it is:-

I have also ordered a death cert for one of the Hollands children. I don't normally do that for distant cousins so hope it tells me something interesting.

Cockett
17. posted 10 May 2018, 18:56

The main benefit of the 1939 census is it has dates of birth!! Apart from that not much use.

Another cousin marriage. This took me a while to establish as the wedding doc for Fanny Hoad as it had her as either marrying a Richard Dalby or a Charles Winton in 1897. This does not tie in with the 1911 census or the births of her children; William George Cockett was born in 1895 and Mabel Rose Cockett was born in 1898. I am still not sure she married Alfred as he dies in 1914 and Fanny is supposed to be a widow in 1911.

Whatevs - William George Cockett married an Elsie Cockett in 1936 in Hastings. Elsie is the daughter of Albert Cockett who might be the brother of Williams father.

Nelson Hoad
18. posted 10 May 2018, 20:46

Nelson Hoad was the son of an ag lab. He was born on the 18th June 1836 in Ashburnham, Sussex and baptised on the 16th October. He lived with his family until at least 1851 and then there appears to be no trace of him in 1861. However, he is in London in the 1860s because that is where he marries Charlotte French and their children are born. Their first daughter appears to have been born out of wedlock, about 4 years before they married. She also has a strange name; Remia. Remia is only found on the 1871 census. The interesting thing about Nelson is he was a hairdresser. After generations of ag labs staying around their villages in Sussex, one gets to London and has a trade.

Nelson may or may not have also married a Sarah Semark in Gravesend in 1860.

Pianoforte
19. posted 10 May 2018, 21:16

At present I have 4.5 Nelson Hoads in my tree. First one mentioned already. Then there is his son (this post) and his grandson, Nelson James Campbell, born 1910. Then there is the nephew of the first one, born 1860 and then he also has a nephew.

Nelson number 2.

Nelson Hoad was born in London in 1871, the son of a hairdresser. His father must have made a comfortable living as a hairdresser because the family had a governess in 1881. The Hoad family lived at 2 Caroline Place, Wirtemburg Street in Clapham. This address does not seem to exist anymore. Nelson had some interesting and it would seem, influential neighbours. Living at no 1 there was a family of teachers including a music teacher. Living at no 3 is a music professor.

By 1891, for some reason Nelson had moved to Canton in Glamorgan. He was working as a pianoforte tuner and was in lodgings. By 1901 he had moved to Llanelly, Carmarthenshire, again in lodgings. He was living with a widow called Annie Thomas and her children. In 1903, Nelson married Annie. He lived in Llanelly until he died in 1935.

Trueman
20. posted 10 May 2018, 22:06

New match for me:-

Predicted relationship: 4th Cousins
Possible range: 4th - 6th cousins Confidence: Good

DNA Match

14

4th cousin
DNA mother
mother of DNA Match
Stanley Harrison (1911 -)
father of DNA mother
George Arthur Harrison (1891 -)
father of Stanley Harrison
Fanny Robinson (1860 - 1936)
mother of George Arthur Harrison
Trueman Robinson (1817 - 1891)
father of Fanny Robinson
George Robinson (1844 - 1907)
son of Trueman Robinson
Alice Robinson (1870 - 1940)
daughter of George Robinson

Moor
21. posted 13 May 2018, 15:09

Another Trueman match today, from the same line as the one from the other day:-

Predicted relationship: Distant Cousins
Possible range: 5th - 8th cousins
Confidence: Moderate

My DNA in the Storm line obviously gets very watered down as the predictions are generally not that good:-

DNA Match
3rd cousin 1x removed
Edith Mary Harrison (1919 - 2012)
mother of DNA Match
George Arthur Harrison (1891 -)
father of Edith Mary Harrison
Fanny Robinson (1860 - 1936)
mother of George Arthur Harrison

Trueman Robinson (1817 - 1891)
father of Fanny Robinson
George Robinson (1844 - 1907)
son of Trueman Robinson
Alice Robinson (1870 - 1940)
daughter of George Robinson

This DNA Match has got a decent tree so in addition to the match via
the Robinson line, we also have a match in the Storm line:-

DNA Match
6th cousin 1x removed
Edith Mary Harrison (1919 - 2012)
mother of DNA Match
George Arthur Harrison (1891 -)
father of Edith Mary Harrison
George Storm Harrison (1859 - 1906) m Fanny Robinson
3rd cousin 4x removed
Mary Storm (1829 - 1900)
mother of George Storm Harrison
John Storm (1801 -)
father of Mary Storm
John Storm (1769 - 1845)
father of John Storm
John Storm (1740 - 1813)
father of John Storm
Elizabeth Storm (1771 - 1846)
daughter of John Storm
John Hodgson Storm (1791 - 1861)
son of Elizabeth Storm
Betsey (Elizabeth) Storm (1814 - 1883)
daughter of John Hodgson Storm
Mary Ann Wickham (1843 - 1916)
daughter of Betsey (Elizabeth) Storm
Alice Robinson (1870 - 1940)
daughter of Mary Ann Wickham

Dependent on the route, the match is either my 3rd cousin 1x removed or my
6th cousin 1x removed. It was a bit mad seeing shared ancestor hint 2 of 2.

This second route would also apply to the match from the other day - so if they were 4th cousin, I suppose that would also make them a 5th cousin too or 4th cousin 1x removed? I wonder if they know each other? What a coincidence that they did tests so close together.

The other interesting thing about this match is the names for John Storm. 1769 John is called John 'Auld Stormy' Storm and 1800 John is called John Attaliah Jack Storm. I doubt I will find out about the nickname, but I want to know if Attaliah was actually a real name documented somewhere.

Another
22.posted 13 May 2018, 15:35

Close relative that I know has done a test.

Predicted relationship: 1st Cousins
Possible range: 1st - 2nd cousins
Confidence: Extremely High

They are my 1st cousin 1x removed, so prediction is good.

Pell
23. posted 13 May 2018, 23:19

Thick n fast on my tree today!

Predicted relationship: Distant Cousins
Possible range: 5th - 8th cousins
Confidence: Moderate

I have not done any of the Pell cousins, so this line is new from Joseph Pell (1809). I did not have anything on him and now he has two wives and I am unsure which one is the mother of Sarah Pell. Anyway:-

DNA Match
5th cousin 1x removed

Turner
parent of DNA Match
David Ross Turner (1943 - 1990)
father of Turner
Florence Ball (1900 - 1974)
mother of David Ross Turner
Joseph Mottram Ball (1864 -)
father of Florence Ball
Sarah Pell (1840 -)
mother of Joseph Mottram Ball
Joseph Pell (1809 -)
father of Sarah Pell
Robert Pell (1766 -)
father of Joseph Pell
George Pell (1799 - 1866)
son of Robert Pell
Frances Pell (1843 - 1924)
daughter of George Pell
Hannah Turfitt (1879 - 1950)
daughter of Frances Pell

Damaris
24. posted 14 May 2018, 06:51

The two Robinson matches made me look at a lot of Storm hints yesterday.
One that interested me was regarding a Mercy Storm Steel. As if Storm wasn't
a cool enough name, they added Steel to the mix. Mercy didn't really do much
to warrant a post, I just liked her name.

Mercy was located because she had a Damaris staying with her. This is also
an unusual name. There are 4 so far.

Damaris Harrison (1788-1839) and she married James Storm.

They have two granddaughters; Damaris Harrison Steel (1849-1935) and
Damaris Harrison Bedlington (1853-1941).

Then they have a great granddaughter from the Bedlington line; Damaris Bedlington Harrison (1889-1974).

All of the men are master mariners/ship owners. I quite liked a census doc for Mercy that describes her as a *'Shipowners daughter'*. Unusually specific.

Neanderthal
25. posted 14 May 2018, 10:15

Yesterday I contacted my cousin to discuss his DNA results and also mention the 1939 register being available.

It turns out that I saw his result before he did! The interesting thing is he has already done a DNA test before, with 23andme. They are the more expensive ones that give you details of genetic illnesses. Nice to know he doesn't have any. However, more importantly, I wanted to know how the ethnicity estimate compared. 23andme is more specific. Where Ancestry will say 'Western Europe', they will say 'France & Germany' but apart from that they are similar.

However, the other part of the test that I didn't know about is cool. It gives you a report on how many Neanderthal variants are in your DNA. Apparently, he has 294 Neanderthal variants which is 77% more than (presumably the average?) other 23andme customers. Apparently, these variants make up less than 4% of our DNA. There are 4 variants that they look at:-

a) Straight Hair (I don't know if that means you are more Neanderthal if you have curly hair or straight hair)

b) Less likely to sneeze after eating dark chocolate (bizarre - and again, which way round?)

c) Less back hair (again I would have thought they were hairier so which way round?)

d) Height (they are shorter, so I assume that is what they are aiming for here)

So of course, I now want to get a test done with 23andme.

Being that I am a short person with straight hair (no idea about the chocolate as I don't like dark), I want to know how Neanderthal I am. On both my maternal and paternal sides the men have back hair. Much to their annoyance.

I shall be monitoring price and I will order when I see it is on offer. Bit scared about finding out about any potential genetic illnesses though.

Variants
26. posted 14 May 2018, 20:03

From what a google has established, all Eurasian people will have 2-4% Neanderthal DNA and if you

Have straight hair
Don't sneeze after eating dark chocolate
Don't have back hair
Are short

you are a bit Neanderthal.

Mad about the back hair. That would indicate my family are not Neanderthal but we are from Europe so we must be.

Sophia Venns
27. posted 15 May 2018, 19:59

I have several Stephen Carley's in my tree. One is my 4th Great Uncle, baptised in Dallington on the 16th October 1794 and was buried on the 30th September 1827 at Hanover Chapel General Burial Ground in Brighton.

Because he died before a census, I couldn't find anything out about him. I did establish that he married a Sophia Venns in 1816 but I had her name as Sophy Venes (due to the Christening doc). They also had three daughters.

I have received a tip from my cousin who told me about the Onion Pie murder about this line that I will try and type up tonight. I do now know why I could not locate Sophie and her daughters after the death of Stephen. She remarried but I cannot find a wedding doc.

Evans
28. posted 16 May 2018, 17:48

yay! Cecilia Evans line appears to be a match!

Predicted relationship: 4th Cousins
Possible range: 4th – 6th cousins
Confidence: Good

DNA Match
4th cousin
Sheila Malcolm
mother of DNA Match
Elizabeth Davies
mother of Sheila Malcolm
Harriet Thomas (1868 -)
mother of Elizabeth Davies
Elizabeth Evans (1845 -)
mother of Harriet Thomas
Daniel Evans (1810 – 1853)
father of Elizabeth Evans
Cecilia Evans (1835 – 1914)
daughter of Daniel Evans
Harriet King (1865 -)
daughter of Cecilia Evans

In other news, the death cert for Hannah Hollands turned up. She died of scarlet fever. I assume her siblings died of the same.

Henry Knox
29. posted 16 May 2018, 18:51

Harriet Thomas married Benjamin Davies in Stockton in 1889 and they went on to have at least 5 daughters including one called Sarah Jane in 1892.

Benjamin died in 1897. Harriet remarried to a widower, Henry Knox. Henry already had at least 4 children with his previous wife Margaret. Harriet and Henry went on to have at least 3 children of their own (public trees have many more) until she died in 1908.

In 1909, Henry married for the third time, this time to a Sarah Jane Davies. I know the name is common, but I really believe he married his step daughter. They had a daughter.

Just eww. Even if not stepfather, he was 45 and she was 17.

James Carley
30. posted 16 May 2018, 19:14

James Carley is the son of Stephen Carley and Sophia Venns. He was baptised in Cranbrook on the 18th June 1820. His father Stephen died when he was just 7 years old. His mother remarried to a William Dorney in 1830.

On the 12th September 1838, James was tried at Lewes for larceny and he was acquitted. Then on the 16th December 1843 he was again at Lewes Court, this time for burglary. He was found guilty and sentenced to 21 years transportation.

On the 13th March 1844 he was put on the ship Blundell to go to the Van Diemens Land colony in Tasmania. James arrived at the colony on the 12th July 1844. He appears on 7 convict muster records. He appears to have been 'pardoned' in the mid-1850s and he married another convict, Mary Wyatt, on

22

the 28th March 1855 at Hobart in Tasmania. James and Mary went on to
have at least 6 children. James died on the 26th December 1917 in Little Bay,
New South Wales.

Mary Wyatt
31. posted 16 May 2018, 19:32

Forgot to mention that James Carley was a tailor. On to his wife.

Mary was born in Whitestaunton, Somerset and baptised their on the 1st
March 1829. On the 14th October 1845, aged 16, she was on trial for larceny
at Somerset. She was acquitted. Four months later, on the 12th January 1846,
she is on trial again, this time for 'larceny by a servant'. She was found guilty
and sentenced to 6 months imprisonment.

On the 29th June 1852, she is on trial again at Somerset. There appear to be
3 charges against her:-

Firstly, she appears to get 6 months for 'broken victuals'. The main charge of
'receiving 2 pigs' gets her 7 years transportation.

The other weird charge is 'Being found in bed with a Lodger on her Masters
premises' for which she appears to have been given 9 months hard labour. I
am really not sure what crime was committed there; it might have been against
her employers wishes but I think it is strange to be sentenced to hard labour
for sleeping with somebody.

Anyway - receiving stolen pigs sent her to Tasmania and she left on the 25th
November 1852. The vessel transporting her was the Duchess of
Northumberland. She arrived at the colony on the 21st April 1853. Her
occupation is given as a 'dairymaid' - presumably at the time of conviction.
As per last post she married and had kids.

Mary died on the 3rd October 1904 in Annandale, New South Wales.

Stephen Carley

32. posted 16 May 2018, 20:05

Stephen Carley was born in Waterloo, NSW on the 24th September 1865, son of James and Mary. On the 14th September 1894, he was tried for 'malicious gbh' at Darlinghurst in NSW. However, the jury failed to deliver a verdict so he was released the next day.

Stephen married Sarah Fielder in 1900 and he died in Marrickville on the 21st May 1912.

Joseph Carley
33. posted 16 May 2018, 21:07

Joseph Carley was born in Newcastle, NSW on the 8th February 1871. On the 28th December 1892, he was arrested for murder:-

"Sydney - Alexander Ross, charged with causing, and Samuel Matthews. Joseph Carley, Adam James Willis, Edward Burden, Frederick Edgerton Diamond, David Hennessy and Emile Kagonnson, charged with being concerned in, causing the death of Alexander Stewart or Davidson at a prize fight, on the 17th instant in York street, Sydney, have been arrested by ....."   New South Wales, Australia, Police Gazettes, 1854-1930

They all appear to have been convicted of the lesser charge of manslaughter on the 2nd March 1893 and all went to Darlinghurst Gaol except for Emile who went to 'the custody of the sheriff'. It is unclear how long they were sentenced for.

Joseph was definitely out of jail before 1899, just 6 years later, because he marries Mary Russell in Sydney. Joseph died in NSW in 1929.

Hallaway
34. posted 17 May 2018, 20:34

John Hallaway was born c1778 in Penshurst, Sussex. In 1798 he had moved to Brightling and was renting land from Thomas Comyns. John appears to be renting 3 areas of land, but I can't read the addresses. They cost £15 2s, £1 4s and £2 8s.

On the 13th December 1815 he married Sophia Carley at St Clements in Hastings. John and Sophia had at least 7 children. By 1842, John is a landowner as he appears on the poll books. He is listed as the owner of Socknersh which is 'freehold house lands and manor'. I have just googled 'Socknersh Manor' and it was once owned by Tom Jones and Englebert Humperdinck! It is an amazing building. I cannot believe that my 1st cousin 5x removed lived there. And her children, my 2nd cousins 4x removed.

On the 1851 census, John is described as a farmer of 400 acres employing 12 labourers, 3 servants and 1 assistant, Sophia Perry. His sister Elizabeth lives with them. She is described as a 'lunatic', but it was probably dementia.

I am not sure what happens to John after that, he seems to appear in another poll book in 1856 but there is also a death doc for a year earlier. I really want to find a probate document to see how much money that gaff was worth. And who he left it to.

In 1859, his son Jesse marries the assistant, Sophia Perry. Then they move to Dodge, Minnesota the following year.

Socknersh
35. posted 17 May 2018, 20:41

I liked this from Country Life July 3, 2014:-

"It's hard to imagine a setting more idyllic than that of historic, Grade II-listed Socknersh Manor -currently for sale through Knight Frank (020-7629 8171) at a guide price of 'excess £5 million'-which sits high on a quiet hillside between Brightling and Burwash in the heart of the Sussex Weald, overlooking a peaceful wooded valley a few miles inland from the coastal towns of Hastings and Pevensey.

This part of Sussex is renowned for its grand houses and large estates, many of them, including Socknersh, created after the Conquest, when the Normans took over the lands of the defeated Saxons. The story of Socknersh Manor begins with Robert de St Leger, who is said to have held out his arm to support William the Conqueror as he stepped off his ship at Pevensey Bay in 1066. The St Leger family, who owned Robertsbridge Abbey in Kent, became the fourth biggest landowners after the King, and Robert's grandson, Rogo, was given the Socknersh estate, and adopted the name of de Socknersh.

All was well until 1215, when the de Socknersh family aligned themselves with the rebel barons against King John. The then Rogo de Socknersh was offered a pardon by the new king, Henry III, but he refused, and was hung, drawn and quartered in the Tower of London. Socknersh was held by the St Legers and their heirs until the 14th century, after which it passed to another ancient Sussex family, the de Boxhulls. An article on Socknersh Manor in Country Life (November 26, 1904) highlights the tranquility of its location 'quiet as it is in this sequestered backwater of the stream of Sussex existence' and the beauty of the surrounding countryside, 'abounding in well-timbered and precipitous hills and dales, among the fairest in this fair county'.

More than 100 years on, little has changed here, and, as the writer suggests, 'it is hard to imagine that busy human life once peopled these sleepy hollows, huge furnaces flared to heaven, hammers clanged, and the iron-workers passed briskly to and from about their

26

business. Great guns were forged in these places, and the cannon that roared out at the Armada, and bombarded La Rochelle, and resounded at Edgehill, were cast in these parts of Sussex'.

In medieval times, the Weald was covered with forests, much of which was cut to feed the furnaces of the ironworks that were the source of the area's wealth from the 13th to the 18th century. The furnace at Socknersh, which operated between about 1525 and 1675, was probably built by John Ashburnham, who also owned a furnace in Ashburnham and a forge in Penshurst. John Collins, the first of the Collins dynasty of Socknersh ironmasters, bought the Socknersh furnace from Ashburnham, and the family moved to Manor Farm, where, in the early 1600s, the present manor house was built, presumably by the wealthy Capt. Thomas Collins JP, a rigid Presbyterian and a loyal Parliamentarian, who inherited Socknersh on his father's death in 1612. He was later one of about 20 sequestrators for Sussex appointed by Cromwell to seize the estates of Royalists who had fought on the wrong side during the Civil War.

The last of the Collins family to live at Socknersh was Henry Collins, who died childless in 1753, leaving the estate to his cousin George. Thereafter, the property was sold several times and, according to an article in The Sussex County Magazine in 1934, 'Socknersh- like other old houses- passed through an epoch of sad neglect when it was used as a farmhouse', before being rescued by Mrs. Odo Cross, who had bought it in a state of disrepair some years before. Then, as now, the house, set at the end of its long tree-lined drive, surprised the visitor 'with its mottled many-patterned walls of red brick… mostly laid herringbone fashion bet- ween the silver-toned beamwork'.

Acting as her own architect, Mrs. Cross made a number of skillful alterations to the manor, taking great care to retrieve and restore as many original elements as possible. The south entrance of the house leads into a very large room, only half of which is old. The rest, including a bay window on the south side, was added by Mrs. Cross. She also added a servants' wing to the oldest part of the house, which had probably been damaged by fire."

http://www.countrylife.co.uk/property/country-houses-for-sale-and-property-news/a-sussex-weald-estate-58115

Burwash

36. posted 19 May 2018, 09:27

Today I have found a little extension to the Snelling line. I had the mother of Anne Langridge as Lucy, but I think her surname is Cruttenden.

John Cruttenden (1670 -)
8th great-grandfather
John Cruttenden (1720 -)
son of John Cruttenden
Lucy Cruttenden (1751 -)
daughter of John Cruttenden
Anne Langridge (1788 -)
daughter of Lucy Cruttenden
William Snelling (1822 - 1855)
son of Anne Langridge
John B Snelling (1844 - 1886)
son of William Snelling
William Alfred Snelling (1873 - 1912)
son of John B Snelling

I have not found the connection between this Cruttenden family and my existing ones in the Green line. They must be connected as the Green line comes from Etchingham in Sussex and these ones are from Burwash. These two villages are only 4 miles away from each other. A little reminder of the Green line:-

Henry Cruttenden (1588 -)
10th great-grandfather
Thomas Cruttenden (1629 -)
son of Henry Cruttenden
Thomas Cruttenden (1661 -)
son of Thomas Cruttenden
Joseph Cruttenden (1700 -)
son of Thomas Cruttenden
Mary Cruttenden (1731 -)
daughter of Joseph Cruttenden
Ann Geall (1765 - 1845)
daughter of Mary Cruttenden

Oxford
37. posted 20 May 2018, 09:45

I believe John Cruttenden born c1694 in Burwash went to Oxford and became a lawyer. (There are 3 John Cruttendens born at this time so even if not my Gt Grandfather, will be an Uncle.)

On the subject of *Suits...* was the Royal Wedding yesterday and it was a tad mad to see Louis Litt in the congregation. (Plus other cast members)

Coat of Arms
38. posted 20 May 2018, 10:05

Not for use by me of course as not my surname/direct descendant/or male but it is nice to know one of my lines had/has a coat of arms.

Some stuff on these sites:-

http://www.surnamedb.com/Surname/Cruttenden

http://www.cruttendenfamily.talktalk.net/surname.htm

I had seen this as a hint on a few trees but I am always seeing coats of arms in trees when they are wrong (same surname does not equal coat of arms!) but I am pretty sure the person who got this is a direct ancestor of me.

Anthony Cruttenden

39. posted 20 May 2018, 11:40

As far as I can tell, the coat of arms was given to Anthony who is not in my tree. Meh.

Anyway, back to people who are in my tree. Elizabeth Geall Westgate (1856-1947) daughter of Samuel Westgate and Mary Geall married her cousin, George Geall. He was the son of Trayton Geall (brother of Mary) and Mary Hallett.

George Geall was in the Royal Navy. He was apparently on *Superb* in 1881 but that ship is not on his record. According to his record he served from 1884 to 1894 and he was on *Penelope, Hotspur, Wildfire, Hotspur* again, *Bellusle* and *Melampus*. His conduct was 'very good' and he was promoted to Acting 2nd Mate on the 2nd February 1894.

In 1901, George is a 'cowman' and in 1911 he is a Naval Office Pensioner. He died in 1930.

Xerxes
40. posted 20 May 2018, 20:14

Nothing interesting other than names.

William Snelling Ratcliff married Lettuce Adine White at St Andrews in Holborn on the 26th April 1880.

What sort of a name is Lettuce???

They had at least 3 children, the boys also having unusual middle names; Ivy Snelling, Harold Elvy and Reginald Xerxes. Wouldn't have a clue how to pronounce that.

British Columbia
41. posted 21 May 2018, 20:18

John Ratcliff was born in 1849 in Shoreham. In 1871 he works as an assistant at his Mums pub. Eliza Ratcliffe (nee Snelling) was the landlady of *the Jolly Fisherman* at 35 Market Street. He married Blanche Marguerite La Croix in 1872 in Brighton. John's occupation in 1881 is 'Gentleman'. I am not sure how you become a Gentleman without inheriting money. Maybe he lied. Maybe he did inherit from someone. In 1891 he is working as an 'Egg and Butter Merchant'. He is not located in 1901 but in 1911 he has fallen further down the social ladder and is now a 'Kitchen Porter'. Blanche is living with their children in 1901. John and Blanche had 15 children, 2 of which had died before 1911. They always lived in Brighton.

It is not clear what happened to John after 1911. Blanche plus 5 of her children emigrated to Victoria in British Columbia. Blanche was born on the 18th November 1853 at St Helier. Think she is first from my tree to be from the Channel Islands. She arrived in Quebec on the 12th September 1923. Blanche died on the 8th July 1934.

Joachim Antonio De Macedo was born in Leeds on the 8th June 1840. He married Carolina, a British Subject born in Cadiz, c1873. I think they might have been married in Portugal as that is where the first of their children were born. Ancestry does not have records for Spain or Portugal. Again, more country firsts.

In 1891, Joachim was working as the 'Portuguese High Counsel'. He was still doing this in 1901 but in addition he was also a wine merchant. Then there is no trace of him or Carolina until 1921 when they are living in Victoria, BC. Joachim died on the 21st March 1922 and Carolina died on the 19th October 1943, both in Victoria, BC.

Worth noting that the only blood in this post is John Ratcliff (and his Mum). There is a John Ratcliff that dies in Brighton in 1927. Maybe Blanche left him. There are several immigration and emigration documents with various John Ratcliff's but they are definitely different people, so it is hard to say what if any journeys he made. He might well have gone to Canada and come back again. One of his grandchildren born in Canada comes to Sussex, marries and stays in England.

The De Macedo's are the in-laws of John and Blanches girls. So nonblood but interesting. The girls will be in the next post.

When?
42. posted 22 May 2018, 22:52

There is a severe lack of Canadian immigration documents on the Ratcliff family. I think that they probably went there c1911 based on these notes:-

Blanche Marguerite La Croix PREVIOUS ENTRY MAY 1911 left Canada 'to visit my children' returned 12 Sep 1923 Ship Name Empress of France Nearest relative in country from which you came :- 'John Ratcliff Husband 25 Market Street Brighton'

Blanche Marie Elise Ratcliff before marriage 2 Dec 1916

Albert John Ratcliffe 1897 (age 12) according to 1921 census

Charles Edward Ratcliff before marriage 1927

Edward Joseph Ratcliff orig dates illeg Aug 18 18??/Dec 24 18?? return 1921 Ship Name Melita

Elise Josephine Ratcliff 1913 (age 20) according to 1921 census

May Augusta Ratcliff before marriage 10 Aug 1914

Mabel Ratcliff 1912 (age 16) according to 1921 census

Interesting that in 1923 Blanche lists her husband as still being in Brighton. They have separated really.

Marie Ratcliff
43. posted 22 May 2018, 23:25

Marie Eugenie Ratcliff was born in Brighton in 1887. She is not located in 1901 but is living with her family in 1911. Marie appears to have stayed in

England when her family went to Canada. I think she must have been a nurse or something in WW1 as she gets married in Paris on the 4th August 1917. Marie marries a Captain in the Army Service Corps; Christopher Frederick Grenside. It is very interesting what she puts in the 'Father in law' section of the marriage document. It says "mother - Mrs. Ratcliff living in Brownholme BC". It is 1917, we know that John is still alive in 1923. Why did she not put John Ratcliff living in Brighton in that part? This family seems very estranged.

They return to England after the war living in Chelsea and then in Berkshire. Christopher died on the 16th February 1938 and he left £1,523 2s 1d between his wife Marie and a Mary Grenside, presumably his sister.

At some point she then goes to visit her family in Canada. She returns to Liverpool on the Empress of Scotland on the 29th September 1950.

Marie died on the 2nd June 1962. She left £2,917 3s in her will.

Treadmill
44. posted 24 May 2018, 10:33

I generally go on the same treadmill at the gym if it is available as I thought it is useful for the Fitbit stats just in case a different machine gives different figures. Last night I did a sad thing and typed up my jog n training times at the gym. I have recently done a couple of 20 mins at 8.5km/hr and they came up as 2.86km and today I did a 30 mins at 8.5km/hr but instead of it being 4.29km, it was 4.22km. I am sure I was on the same treadmill. I think my stats are therefore not entirely accurate. What is for definite is that I have improved since February. I would never have been able to do 30 mins continuously at 8.5 back then. Initially any jogging stints would have been at 8 and then I did increase that to 8.3. 8.5 is definitely my favourite pace, 8.7 I cannot sustain for very long, I can only do 9 or 9.5 for a very short time.

75
45. posted 24 May 2018, 20:52

I have been watching the weather for Monday. It has steadily been getting warmer and today the forecast has changed to include storms. Not sure about running outside. Anyway, assuming the weather is dry with a nice breeze, I would like to say I will do 10k in 75 mins, but I reckon it is going to be 80. Here is what I have been doing jogging wise this year. Considering I have never ever jogged in the previous 46 years, I am quite impressed with myself. (The last two entries are in the future)

I haven't actually sped up as much as it might seem, most of the s25k 'runs' start with a 5 min walk.

5k train	Duration	Distance	Average	
03/02/2018	Walk/Run	44.21	5.00	8.84
05/02/2018	S25K Week 5 Run1	26.00	3.00	8.67
07/02/2018	S25K Week 5 Run1	26.00	3.10	8.39
09/02/2018	S25K Week 5 Run1	26.00	3.08	8.44
12/02/2018	S25K Week 6 Run1	29.00	3.45	8.41
13/02/2018	Walk/Run	42.40	5.00	8.48
16/02/2018	S25K Week 5 Run2	26.00	3.21	8.10
19/02/2018	S25K Week 5 Run2	26.00	3.10	8.39
21/02/2018	S25K Week 5 Run2	26.00	3.15	8.25
24/02/2018	S25K Week 6 Run2	28.00	3.40	8.24
26/02/2018	Walk/Run	38.42	5.00	7.68
27/02/2018	S25K Week 6 Run2	28.00	3.44	8.14
28/02/2018	S25K Week 5 Run3	25.00	3.18	7.86
05/03/2018	S25K Week 5 Run3	25.00	3.11	8.04
12/03/2018	S25K Week 6 Run2	28.00	3.44	8.14
14/03/2018	S25K Week 5 Run3	25.00	3.09	8.09
15/03/2018	S25K Week 6 Run3	30.00	3.81	7.87
16/03/2018	Walk/Run	39.02	5.00	7.80
17/03/2018	Run	15.00	2.12	7.08
18/03/2018	S25K Week 6 Run2	28.00	3.66	7.65
24/03/2018	Run	15.00	2.10	7.14
25/03/2018	Run	15.00	2.22	6.76
26/03/2018	S25K Week 5 Run3	25.00	3.24	7.72
27/03/2018	S25K Week 7 Run	30.00	3.84	7.81
28/03/2018	S25K Week 7 Run	30.00	3.89	7.71
02/04/2018	Run	36.19	5.00	7.24
03/04/2018	S25K Week 8 Run	33.00	4.49	7.35

Date	Activity		Duration	Distance	Average
04/04/2018	Run	15.00	2.22	6.76	
06/04/2018	S25K Week 9 Run		35.00	4.63	7.56
07/04/2018	Run	36.01	5.00	7.20	
09/04/2018	Run	15.22	not rec		
10/04/2018	Run (outside)	32.25	not rec		
12/04/2018	Run	17.04	not rec		
14/04/2018	South London 5K		36.59	5.00	7.32
	Post 5k Duration				
18/04/2018	Run	17.04	not rec		
25/04/2018	Run	20.29	not rec		
26/04/2018	Run	29.52	not rec		
10k train	Duration		Distance		Average
30/04/2018	10k 4wtg Run2	53.00	7.19	7.37	
01/05/2018	10k 4wtg Run3	70.00	9.28	7.54	
03/05/2018	10k 4wtg Run1	35.00	4.46	7.85	
05/05/2018	10k 4wtg Run1	35.00	4.93	7.10	
08/05/2018	10k 3wtg Run1	40.00	5.51	7.26	
10/05/2018	10k 3wtg Run2	59.00	8.11	7.27	
12/05/2018	10k 3wtg Run3	70.00	9.50	7.37	
15/05/2018	10k 2wtg Run1	20.00	2.86	6.99	
17/05/2018	10k 2wtg Run2	56.00	7.63	7.34	
20/05/2018	10k 2wtg Run3	50.00	6.96	7.18	
22/05/2018	10k 1wtg Run2	20.00	2.86	6.99	
24/05/2018	10k 1wtg Run1	30.00	4.29	6.99	
26/05/2018	10k 1wtg Run3	15.00	2.15	6.99	
28/05/2018	Vitality 10k	75.00	10.00	7.50	

De Macedo
46. posted 24 May 2018, 21:35

Louis Ernest De Macedo was born in Leeds on the 21st June 1881. Louis emigrated to Canada with his family, arriving in the US on the 26th January 1908. He married May Augusta Radcliff in Canada on the 10th August 1914.

On the 10th February 1919, he signed up for WW1. (date seems strange, maybe a leaving document?) Louis worked as a clerk. He is described as 5ft 5 3/4" tall, a dark complexion, brown eyes and light brown hair. He had mild varicose veins in his right leg and was a Catholic. According to the attestation doc he had served in the Royal Air Force for 9 months but the document is on Fold3 so I cannot view it. Louis and May had at least one child.

Joachim Anthony Augustine De Macedo is one of Louis' brothers. He was born in Leeds on the 8th April 1879. He appears to marry in 1901 in Tadcaster. Not sure what happened to his wife if he did. Joachim married Blanche Marie Elise Radcliff in Canada on the 2nd December 1916. (Blanche is the sister of May). Like his brother, he also served in the Royal Air Force, his service record on Fold3 has a date of 29th June 1917. Clues on his Canadian doc though. Joachim had spent two years in the 4th Battalion of the West Yorkshire Regiment, a Lieutenant in the Royal Flying Corps for 1 year and 2 months. He had also been in a Canadian Regiment for 4 months, the Gordon Highlanders.

His attestation document is dated 25th February 1919. Joachim was an 'Intensive Horticulturalist'. He is described as 5ft 3 1/2" tall, a dark complexion, hazel eyes and brown hair. He had a mole on his right forearm and is obviously Catholic like his brother. Joachim died on the 14th January 1928 in Victoria, BC.

Vitality 10k
47. posted 28 May 2018, 16:09

This was a really cool route. Start in Green Park, go to Trafalgar Square, onwards to St Paul's, then back again, finishing off outside Buckingham Palace. Apparently, there were around 17,000 people. It was certainly different to the South London 5k where there was plenty of space. It was quite packed and frequently having to dodge round people. I didn't stop for a walk after I got to the 5k mark as I expected to. I carried on. After 7k I would say my legs were tired and I thought in my head that I must be slowing down. I had a little walk at 9k (didn't even register on the Fitbit so just a few steps at walk pace really). Then bizarrely I found some energy just before the finish line and actually ran to it.

Scores on the doors - 1 hour 14mins 48 secs - 74.48 - so very surprised that I did it under what I thought was an optimistic estimate of 75 mins. I thought because of my lead legs towards the end that it might have been a faster first 5k, but it was 37.11 which is pretty much exactly an even split.

So yeah, been there, done that, literally got the t-shirt. And medal.

Match
48. posted 28 May 2018, 20:34

Husband has a new match that has no shared matches - could that indicate a Paternal clue that isn't Knight? Sadly, no tree. Messaged but not hopeful of finding the connection.

Predicted relationship: 3rd Cousins
Possible range: 3rd - 4th cousins
Confidence: Extremely High

Liverpool
49. posted 3 Jun 2018, 12:17

Half term. Due to a lot of factors, no holiday was booked, and we went to Liverpool for a few days. It was strange and good at the same time. I haven't been to many cities in the UK. Genuinely surprised at how small the city is and how it is not built up. This London girl is used to skyscrapers.

So did the Beatles Museum, went to The Cavern (that was great), went on a ferry across the Mersey and went to see the statues on Crosby beach. A nice break.

Back home and wanting some new DNA hits or just new people to look at. In an Ancestry doldrum again.

Old Skool
50. posted 7 Jun 2018, 19:59

Got a match via a PM and a tree.

> Contact
> **4th cousin 1x removed** of son
> Mother of Contact
> Grandfather of Contact
> Mary A Topliff (1854 -)
> mother of Grandfather of Contact
> Mary Pittard (1830 - 1895)
> mother of Mary A Topliff
> **Henry Pittard (1805 - 1876)**
> father of Mary Pittard
> Sarah Pittard (1833 - 1916)
> daughter of Henry Pittard
> Jessie Tee (1868 -)
> daughter of Sarah Pittard
> William Thomas Gardner (1897 -)
> son of Jessie Tee

I haven't really ever looked at the Pittard or Topliff lines before so going to see if anything interesting turns up.

Jesse Jelly
51. posted 9 Jun 2018, 11:47

Jesse Julia Gardner married Joseph Jelly on the 24th May 1915. I have known this for a very long time. However, the 1939 register is providing some new titbits. Apparently by 1939, Joseph was living with 3 of their children but his marital status is divorced. Interesting but cannot find out anything more about it. Neither of them appear to have remarried.

Clear

52. posted 10 Jun 2018, 10:52

William Clear and Frances Tee married in Warblington, Hampshire on the 26th June 1817. They had at least 5 children including two daughters, Frances (1821) and Louisa (1836).

In 1868, Frances married a George Knight and in 1875, Louisa married a Frank Knight. Can't find an immediate connection between the two Knights.

Frances and George had a daughter Susannah in 1874. Frances had a brother called John Clear. John married Fanny Saunders on the 1st October 1870 in South Bersted. John and Fanny had at least 2 children including a son called Thomas in 1872.

Susannah Knight married Thomas Clear in 1906.

Goodman
53. posted 10 Jun 2018, 18:25

Did a search for Jelly on the boys DNA matches and have had a result:-

Predicted relationship: 4th Cousins
Possible range: 4th - 6th cousins
Confidence: Good

DNA Match Goodman
3rd cousin of son
Goodman
father of DNA Match Goodman
Goodman (1915 -)
father of Goodman
Frederick Ernest Goodman (1888 - 1942)
father of Goodman
Charles Ernest Goodman (1862 - 1921)
father of Frederick Ernest Goodman
Jessie Goodman (1898 -)
daughter of Charles Ernest Goodman

Doreen Joan Fearn (1929 - 1985)
daughter of Jessie Goodman

Tredgett
54. posted 10 Jun 2018, 18:40

Another search with a result, and a very distant one

Predicted relationship: Distant Cousins
Possible range: 5th - 8th cousins
Confidence: Moderate

DNA Match
6th cousin of son
mother of DNA Match
Jeffery
mother of h
Jeffery
father of Jeffery
Charles Jeffery (1864 -)
father of Jeffery
Julia Ann Tredgett (1847 -)
mother of Charles Jeffery
George Tredgett (1823 - 1899)
father of Julia Ann Tredgett
William Tredgett (1788 - 1864)
father of George Tredgett
Charles Tredgett (1811 - 1882)
son of William Tredgett
William Tredgett (1836 - 1903)
son of Charles Tredgett
Alice Melinda Tredgett (1865 - 1949)
daughter of William Tredgett
Jessie Goodman (1898 -)
daughter of Alice Melinda Tredgett

Potential

55. posted 13 Jun 2018, 20:02

Just as you really get bored, Ancestry gets a new feature. I was looking for another Tee to investigate and at the end of the line I saw a green box. It said Potential Father. When you click on it, the suggestion comes up:-

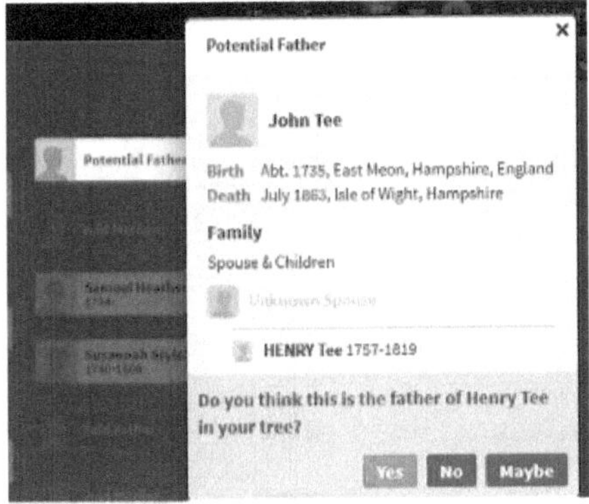

I wonder how it works. Is it a combo of public tree suggestions? Is it from their own Mormon archive? If so - why wouldn't I have found it on Family Search?

It is nice to have something different to investigate. I have been through both trees and there are a few more. I guess people without a tree as comprehensive as mine would have more. Or is it because my trees are so large that I get these new style hints?

On the Green line - possible maiden name for my 7th Great Grandmother

    Again, on Green line, a whole load
    Brain Tucknott line - both parents of Lydia Button
    Knibbs line - both parents of Mary Ann Rice

Of course, there wouldn't be anything on the Paterson line. There are also 3 on the husband's tree. Know what I am doing tonight.

William Barber
56. posted 13 Jun 2018, 23:04

I have been working my way through the Green 'potentials' and have looked at 20 hints so far. I have decided they are Millennium Files. This is because like Millennium Files, they are oddly specific for the dates concerned and there are no docs to back these 'facts' up with. Also, like Millennium Files, some dead ends smack of desperation.

An example of this is William Barber. I know his father is Thomas Barber. The potential mother was :- "Mrs. Thomas Barber Birth ABT 1561,England Death UNKNOWN"

Brilliant.

I am accepting the hints despite this. I know what people are documented and which ones aren't.

63
57. posted 14 Jun 2018, 22:29

Gone through 63 potentials. I wonder if any will have documents to back them up?

Breakdown by line:-

Brain   15
Gardner   1
Green   22
Knibbs   14
Maddox   7

42

Marion Matilda
58. posted 20 Jun 2018, 18:56

Had a decent hint (not a potential) on nephews' line. Always been most frustrated about not getting a maiden name for the husband of Alfred Baker when they got married when docs are available. Anyway - getting her surname of Kemp has allowed me to get back this far:-

George Kemp (1730 -)
7th great-grandfather of nephew
William Kemp (1755 -)
son of George Kemp
William Kemp (1792 - 1871)
son of William Kemp
Edwin Kemp (1833 -)
son of William Kemp
Marion Matilda Kemp (1864 - 1939)
daughter of Edwin Kemp
Evelyn Sara Baker (1900 -)
daughter of Marion Matilda Kemp
Evelyn Maude Violet Saddleton (1920 - 1994)
daughter of Evelyn Sara Baker

Cornwell
59. posted 20 Jun 2018, 19:39

Excellent:-

James Cornwell (1640 -)
10th great-grandfather of nephew
Jeremiah Cornwell (1665 -)
son of James Cornwell
Francis Cornwell (1702 -)

son of Jeremiah Cornwell
Thomas Cornwell (1738 -)
son of Francis Cornwell
Jeremiah Cornwell (1772 -)
son of Thomas Cornwell
Sarah Ann Cornwall (1806 - 1853)
daughter of Jeremiah Cornwell
Edwin Kemp (1833 -)
son of Sarah Ann Cornwall
Marion Matilda Kemp (1864 - 1939)
daughter of Edwin Kemp

Marden
60. posted 21 Jun 2018, 21:38

Some more Kemp extensions and a vision:-

William Relfe (1600 -)
11th great-grandfather of nephew
William Relfe (1634 - 1694)
son of William Relfe
Alice Relfe (1670 -)
daughter of William Relfe
Francis Cornwell (1702 -)
son of Alice Relfe

William Cooper (1620 -)
11th great-grandfather of nephew
Alice Cooper (1640 - 1670)
daughter of William Cooper
Alice Relfe (1670 -)
daughter of Alice Cooper
Francis Cornwell (1702 -)
son of Alice Relfe

Margaret Reeve (1620 -)
11th great-grandmother of nephew

44

Alice Cooper (1640 - 1670)
daughter of Margaret Reeve
Alice Relfe (1670 -)
daughter of Alice Cooper

"*In 1870-72, John Marius Wilson's Imperial Gazetteer of England and Wales described Marden like this:*

MARDEN, a village, a parish, a sub-district, and a hundred, in Kent. The village stands near an affluent of the river Medway, and on the Reigate, Tunbridge, and Ashford railway, 3 miles WNW of Staplehurst; is a picturesque place; was formerly a market town; and has a post office ‡ under Staplehurst, a railway station with telegraph, and a fair on 11 Oct.—The parish contains also the hamlet of Stile-Bridge. ...

*Acres, 7,607. Real property, £11,652. Pop., 2,295. Houses, 452. The property is much subdivided. The manor belongs to R. Springett, Esq. The living is a vicarage in the diocese of Canterbury. Value, £828. * Patron, the Archbishop of Canterbury. The church is ancient but good; consists of nave, aisles, and chancel, with a tower; and contains a very curious font of 1652. There are chapels for Independents and Wesleyans, parochial schools, a Church of England school, and charities £55. The parochial schools were built in 1859, at a cost of about £1,600; and are a handsome structure, in the Tudor style. Amhurst, the author of the "Craftsman, "was a native.—The sub-district contains also two other parishes, and part of another; and is in Maidstone district. Acres, 15,317. Pop. in 1861,4,905. Houses, 906.-The hundred excludes one of the parishes and the part-parish of the subdistrict but includes another and larger parish; and is in the lathe of Scray. Acres, 23,029. Pop. in 1851, 6,550. Houses, 1,227.*"

http://www.visionofbritain.org.uk/place/6273

Stone
61. posted 22 Jun 2018, 22:01

Predicted relationship: 4th Cousins
Possible range: 4th - 6th cousins
Confidence: Good

DNA Match
4th cousin

Curtis
mother of DNA Match
Curtis (1926 -)
Grandfather of DNA Match
William Henry Curtis (1894 - 1929)
father of Curtis
Jane Sophia Stone (1860 - 1932)
mother of William Henry Curtis
Henry Stone (1841 - 1905)
father of Jane Sophia Stone
Alice Elizabeth Stone (1869 - 1953)
daughter of Henry Stone
Annie Louisa Aylen (1891 -)
daughter of Alice Elizabeth Stone

Two Years
62. posted 23 Jun 2018, 09:07

Back to looking at Kemp extensions in the Marden area:-

William Shaw (1670 -)
9th great-grandfather of nephew
Jane Shaw (1706 -)
daughter of William Shaw
Thomas Cornwell (1738 -)
son of Jane Shaw

On a different note, been 2 years since people voted for us to leave. And we STILL have no idea how anything will work. Airbus and BMW have said they are going to leave the UK (with many job losses) if the transition time is not extended. There is however, one thing that has finally been sorted and that was probably about the easiest thing to do... they have announced how EU residents will apply to remain. On the face of it, the solution of 3 simple questions online, should work well. Time will tell.

Relfewere

William Relfe and Bridget had at least 9 children between 1619 and 1638. One of which was William Relfe, baptised on the 25th February 1634 in Goudhurst, Kent. On the 10th May 1670, William married Alice Cooper in Marden. This appears to have been after their daughter Alice was baptised on the 18th January 1670. Alice Cooper died at some point before 1672. This is because William remarries to Jane Cooper on the 29th June 1672 in Wadhurst, Sussex. It does appear that they are sisters. They are the daughters of William Cooper and Margaret Reeve. William and Jane go on to have at least 6 children between 1673 and 1688. One of these is Mary Relfe, baptised in Marsden on the 30th March 1673.

On the 30th October 1694, William Shaw married a Mary Relfewere in Marden. The name was too similar and have subsequently found documents with correct spelling. Therefore, there are two lines feeding into Relfe. Thomas Cornwell (1738) has one Grandmother called Alice Relfe (1670 married Jeremiah Cornwell) and another Grandmother called Mary Relfe (1670 married William Shaw).

Bonny
64. posted 23 Jun 2018, 16:39

Not 100% convinced with the two John Bonney/Bonny in this. Too much moving around Kent. If they are correct, then the line stays in East Sutton and the rest would be right.

Thomas Bonney (1595 -)
11th great-grandfather of nephew
Alexander Bonney (1632 -)
son of Thomas Bonney
Matthew Bonney (1671 -)
son of Alexander Bonney
John Bonney (1708 -)
son of Matthew Bonney
John Bonney (1736 -)
son of John Bonney
Elizabeth Bonney (1765 - 1848)

daughter of John Bonney

"In 1870-72, John Marius Wilson's Imperial Gazetteer of England and Wales described East Sutton like this:

SUTTON (East), a parish in Hollingbourn district, Kent; 3½ miles N of Headcorn r. station. Post town, Staplehurst. Acres, 1,590. Real property, £2,434. Pop., 385. Houses, 74. The manor, with East Sutton Place, belongs to Sir E. Filmer, Bart. The living is a p. curacy, annexed to Sutton-Valence. The church is old and interesting. Charities, £89."

http://www.visionofbritain.org.uk/place/6430

Betty
65.   posted 23 Jun 2018, 17:41

Yesterday we got a puppy. We bought her from our neighbours. She is half English Bulldog (her Mum Flo) and half Cocker Spaniel (her Dad Oscar). She is 8 weeks old, born on the 25th April. I am not sure how I got conned into this. She is lovely and cute, but I have being saying NO for years. About 20 years.

A few more extensions:-

Abraham Earle (1560 -)
12th great-grandfather of nephew
Elizabeth Earle (1597 -)
daughter of Abraham Earle
Alexander Bonny (1632 -)
son of Elizabeth Earle

Abraham Butcher (1600 -)
11th great-grandfather of nephew
Martha Butcher (1634 - 1674)
daughter of Abraham Butcher
Matthew Bonny (1671 -)
son of Martha Butcher

48

Mary Wilson (1600 -)
11th great-grandmother of nephew
Martha Butcher (1634 – 1674)
daughter of Mary Wilson
Matthew Bonny (1671 -)
son of Martha Butcher

Vallentine Bowles
66. posted 24 Jun 2018, 08:46

A few Alfred Baker extensions:-

Thomas Baker (1760 -)
7th great-grandfather of nephew
Thomas Baker (1781 -)
son of Thomas Baker
Thomas Baker (1810 -)
son of Thomas Baker

Olivia Fryer (1780 -)
6th great-grandmother of nephew
Thomas Baker (1810 -)
son of Olivia Fryer

Thomas Garling (1700 -)
8th great-grandfather of nephew
Thomas Garlinge (1735 - 1786)
son of Thomas Garling
Thomas Garling (1773 - 1844)
son of Thomas Garlinge

In addition, also got the surname of Thomasin/Thomazin - it is Bowles, giving her a father of Vallentine Bowles. The 'potential' suggests 'Charles Bowles of Chatham' but I can't confirm that. Neither can a google search:-

Vallentine Bowles (- 1711)
10th great-grandfather of nephew
Thomazin Bowles (1663 -)
daughter of Vallentine Bowles

"Valentine Bowles settled in Deal in the mid-17th Century and became prominent in the early history of the town. He was a Grocer by trade and a member of the committee that secured the Royal Charter for Deal in 1699. His children were baptised at St. Leonard's, Deal, but as a committed Quaker they were also registered at the Friends Meeting House in Folkestone. Unfortunately, Valentine's faith led him into conflict with the authorities for the 'crime' of Recusancy, this being the refusal to attend Church regularly. There are also records of his being briefly incarcerated in Deal Castle. He was married to Elizabeth Cleere the daughter of Tobias Cleere, an Apothecary of Sandwich who was Mayor of that town four times and one of the canopy bearers at the Coronation of Charles II in 1661.

Mystery has always surrounded Valentine Bowles' ancestry and over the years many theories have been suggested, three of which are detailed below.

1) That he was the son of Charles Bowles of Chatham, a wealthy merchant and fellow Quaker and his wife Agnes Cole – Although this is a tempting explanation, there is no mention of a son of this name in his Will of 1659 and the names Charles and Agnes do not appear in Valentine's large family in Deal. However, Charles did have a son called Phineas that mirrors the name of one of Valentine's sons.

2) Another theory is that he was the son of Valentine and Frances Bowle of Rochester – There is very little information about this couple but there is no evidence of a son called Valentine and, again, the name Frances does not appear in Valentine's family.

3) The third popular theory is that he was the son of Valentine Bowles, a wealthy Vintner of London and his wife Elizabeth Isacke – According to Boyd's Inhabitants of London this couple married in 1617 and did indeed had a son called Valentine but this child died in 1627. In his Will published in 1637 Valentine Bowles was survived by his wife Elizabeth and daughters Anne and Elizabeth."

Reference
Boyd's Inhabitants Of London and Family Units 1200-1946
A new Theory

Looking at local records it seems likely that Valentine Bowles may have his roots in a location much closer to Deal than London, Chatham or Rochester. Confusion has possibly arisen because of variations in the spelling of his surname in the Parish Registers, a common occurrence at this time. The earliest reference I can trace for this family is the following marriage in Deal in 1568.

St.Leonard's, Deal
Richard Bowle m Annis Heringe 27 Jul 1568

Richard Bowle was Valentine's Grandfather. Unfortunately, I cannot trace his line back any further. I do believe that Annis had a brother called John who married Elizabeth Reynold in 1676 at St Leonard's, Deal. When John died in 1592, he left a Will that was witnessed by Richard Bowle. He also made a bequest to Agnes Bowle to be paid to her on the day of her marriage.

Richard and Annis Bowle settled in Ringwould where they had the following children

Ringwould
Felix or Phillis? d of Richard 30 Nov 1575
(The transcription gives the name as Felix, but the entry clearly says 'd' for daughter)
Agnes d of Richard 11 Mar 1577
Richard s of Richard 21 Dec 1580
Sarah d of Richard 1 Jan 1581 Bur 25 Dec 1583
Anthony Bowl s of Richard 13 Dec 1584
Margaret d of Richard 19 Nov 1587 Bur 26 Jan 1587
John's of Richard 10 Aug 1589 Bur 23 Jan 1619
Missing baptisms
Richard Bowle s of Richard Bur 29 Sept 1580

(I believe that there are other Baptisms that pre-date the available Parish Register or took place elsewhere).

Richard Bowle died in 1596 and was buried in Ringwould. His wife Annis Bowle was buried there in 1610 where she appears on the Register as follows:-

Mother Bowle Widow Bur 26 Apr 1610

References
St.Leonard's, Deal Parish Register / Find My Past
Ringwould Parish Register / Find My Past
Family Search
Canterbury Cathedral Archives"

http://www.eastkenthistory.org.uk/people:bowles-valentine

Michaels
66. posted 24 Jun 2018, 14:27

Last 2 Alfred Baker extensions:-

Michael Bayly (1620 -)
11th great-grandfather of nephew
Susanna Bayly (1647 -)
daughter of Michael Bayly
Ann Minter (1670 -)
daughter of Susanna Bayly
Michael Cock (1700 -)
son of Ann Minter
Sarah Cock (1740 -)
daughter of Michael Cock
Lydia Court (1783 - 1865)
daughter of Sarah Cock

Michael Minter
11th great-grandfather of nephew
Bartholomew Minter (1645 - 1698)
son of Michael Minter
Ann Minter (1670 -)
daughter of Bartholomew Minter
Michael Cock (1700 -)
son of Ann Minter

Ruardean
67. posted 24 Jun 2018, 19:30
52

Now looking at Brain line extensions. Not 100% sure about William John Yearsley as that was a 'potential' hint. If he is correct, his father is definitely Steven. William John Yearsley also leaves a will and there is a copy but too tired to try and read it tonight.

Steven Yearsley (1590 -)
11th great-grandfather of nephew
William John Yearsley (1625 - 1699)
son of Steven Yearsley
Thomas Yearsley (1670 -)
son of William John Yearsley
Thomas Yearsley (1699 -)
son of Thomas Yearsley
James Yearsley (1745 -)
son of Thomas Yearsley
William Yearsley (1775 - 1841)
son of James Yearsley
Elizabeth Yearsley (1786 - 1851)
daughter of William Yearsley
Ann Knowlson (1821 - 1904)
daughter of Elizabeth Yearsley
Alfred Brain (1848 - 1908)
son of Ann Knowlson

John Nelms (1680 -)
9th great-grandfather of nephew
Sarah Nelms (1706 -)
daughter of John Nelms
James Yearsley (1745 -)
son of Sarah Nelms

This particular line is all Forest of Dean area of Gloucestershire, but I had to lookup Ruardean as never heard of it before.

"In 1870-72, John Marius Wilson's Imperial Gazetteer of England and Wales described Ruardean like this:
RUARDEAN, a parish, with a village, in the district of Ross and county of Gloucester; 4½ miles W by S of Mitcheldean-Road r. station, and 6 N W of Newnham. It has a

post-office under Ross. Acres, 1, 590. Real property, £4, 658; of which £200 are in mines, £47 in quarries, and £220 in ironworks. ...

Pop., 1,054. Houses, 242. The manor belongs to Col. J. Vaughan. There are ruins of an ancient castle. The living is a vicarage in the diocese of Gloucester and Bristol. Value, £100. Patrons, the Ecclesiastical Commissioners. The church is partly Norman and has a tower and spire. There are an Independent chapel, and charities £14."

http://www.visionofbritain.org.uk/place/11150

Kenardington
68. posted 26 Jun 2018, 21:43

There are so many places just an hour away that I have never heard of. The May line come from Kenardington??

George May (1638 -)
9th great-grandfather of nephew
Robert May (1687 -)
son of George May
Margaret May (1714 - 1795)
daughter of Robert May
Joseph Saddleton (1765 - 1842)
son of Margaret May

Margaret Chittenden (1633 -)
9th great-grandmother of nephew
Robert May (1687 -)
son of Margaret Chittenden

"In 1870-72, John Marius Wilson's Imperial Gazetteer of England and Wales described Kenardington like this:

KENARDINGTON, a parish, with a village, in Tenterden district, Kent; near the Royal Military canal, 1½ mile SW of Ham-Street r. station, and 7 SSW of Ashford. Post town, Ham-Street, under Ashford. Acres, 2, 160. Real property, £3, 222. Pop., 221. Houses, 42. Much of the land is occupied with coppice, called Silcox-wood. ...

54

An ancient earthwork is on elevated ground, near the village; is connected, by a narrow causeway, with another ancient earthwork in the marsh below; and these works are supposed by some to have been formed by the ancient British, -by others to have been formed, about 893, during the wars between Alfred and the Danes. The living is a rectory and a vicarage in the diocese of Canterbury. Value, £114. Patron, Mrs. Breton. The church comprises aisle and chancel, with a bell turret; and succeeded one which was destroyed by lightning in 1559."

http://www.visionofbritain.org.uk/place/4494

One of the other children of George and Margaret interested me so I looked at his in-laws to see if they were connected to his indirect descendants. Couldn't see a connection.

Nicholas Saddleton (1650 -)
father-in-law of 9th great-uncle of nephew
Mary Saddleton (1689 -)
daughter of Nicholas Saddleton
George May (1689 -)
husband of Mary Saddleton
George May (1638 -)
father of George May
Robert May (1687 -)
son of George May
Margaret May (1714 - 1795)
daughter of Robert May
Joseph Saddleton (1765 - 1842)
son of Margaret May

I was also interested in

Frances Best (- 1706)
mother-in-law of 9th great-uncle of nephew
Mary Saddleton (1689 -)
daughter of Elisabeth Frances Best
George May (1689 -)
husband of Mary Saddleton

As the baptism hint made her very young when she married but there weren't any others.

Everest
69. posted 1 Jul 2018, 12:54

I have a new hint for Mary Hollands. (Well 2 saying the same thing) They are baptism docs giving her parents as William Hollands and Jane Ribbens. For some reason I have Jane Everest as her mother. The problem with the Saddleton line is it is one that I did pretty much at the beginning so blindly accepted public tree hints. Further investigation required!!

Hollands V2
70. posted 1 Jul 2018, 20:58

Whilst looking at the other issue, I decided the parents of William Hollands were wrong, so I have tree severed it.

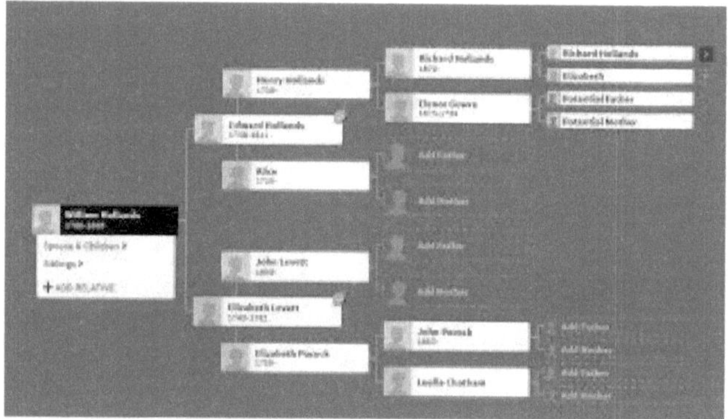

I now believe his parents are David Hollands and Abigail Thomas giving me these lines:-

56

Thomas Ellis (1600 -)
10th great-grandfather of nephew
Christopher Ellis (1644 -)
son of Thomas Ellis
Alice Ellis (1682 -)
daughter of Christopher Ellis
Abigail Acres (1708 -)
daughter of Alice Ellis
Abigail Thomas (1737 - 1816)
daughter of Abigail Acres
William Hollands (1780 - 1865)
son of Abigail Thomas

Bennett Bell (1605 - 1645)
10th great-grandmother of nephew
Christopher Ellis (1644 -)
son of Bennett Bell

Thomasine Cuckow (1660 -)
9th great-grandmother of nephew
Alice Ellis (1682 -)
daughter of Thomasine Cuckow

Simon Acres (1680 - 1744)
8th great-grandfather of nephew
Abigail Acres (1708 -)
daughter of Simon Acres

David Hollands (1738 - 1806)
6th great-grandfather of nephew
William Hollands (1780 - 1865)

The Woodmen of Rough Common
71. posted 2 Jul 2018, 19:46

George Saddleton was born in Harbledown on the 6th October 1811. He was the son of John Saddleton and Celia Wraight. Despite his birth location being Harbledown according to census docs, George was baptised in Ham on the 16th October. I cannot locate Ham, Kent. It is too small a hamlet near Sandwich. But Sandwich is about 15 miles from Harbledown so that seems a bit strange. I wonder whether it is short for Chilham which is 6.1 miles away from Harbledown.

I really want to see this sign in real life!
(from https://en.wikipedia.org/wiki/Ham,_Kent#/media/File:Hamsandwichroadsign.jpg)

But they move around and it might be that he was born in Ham, Sandwich but always lived in Harbledown so that's why he says where he was born. On the 29th November 1834, George married a Mary Hollands. (Looking into George is an attempt to sort out who her parents are - hasn't helped. I would have written up his bio already in 'Mum!...') George and Mary had at least 13 children between 1835 and 1861. They always lived in Harbledown, specifically Rough Common.

George worked as an ag lab until at least 1851. However, by 1861 he was a woodman. He worked as a woodman for the rest of his life though by 1891 he is disabled. George died in 1899 in Harbledown. Mary died in 1906. She was living on her own means in 1901.

More on Harbledown:-
http://harbledownpc.co.uk/parish/local-information/harbledown-and-rough-common-history/

Mary Hollands
72. posted 2 Jul 2018, 21:35

There are three things we KNOW about Mary:-

1. She married George Saddleton on the 29th November 1834 in Harbledown
2. According to census docs she was born in Chilham
3. She died in Harbledown in 1906.

Census docs 1841-1901 give her an average birth year of 1819 - yet that would make her only 14 or 15 in 1834. Based on the census birth year, her most likely parents are William Hollands and Jane Ribbens. This is what one public tree and the 'potential' say. The other public trees say William Hollands and Jane Everest, but she is even younger. Their age is also an issue for their first born. Ribbens 16, Everest 15. Not impossible though. Especially to then go churning them out for next 27 years.

The next issue with Ribbens and Everest is that they gave birth to their Mary Hollands in Eynsford and Edenbridge respectively, both are nowhere near Chilham.

Going by proximity to Chilham, 1812 in Nackington seems likely. But with Harriet there is the reverse problem, she will be 49 when the last child is born.

In the census docs, Mary is always Mary and not Mary Ann. That removes 1813, Hardres. There are two other Mary Ann's.

There are 6 Mary Hollands born in various locations in Kent between 1812 and 1820 and it could be any of them.

Samuel Goddard

73. posted 5 Jul 2018, 22:08

Whilst trying to ascertain a marriage date for him and Margaret, (unsuccessful)
I stumbled upon this:-

http://discovery.nationalarchives.gov.uk/details/r/C10384281

A report he made about some chap that died who refused to go to the
workhouse.

Croatia
74. posted 11 Jul 2018, 18:44

It is all a bit exciting in England this evening. The World Cup semifinal is
due to start in about 15 mins - England v Croatia. Will we reach a final for
the first time since 1966?

Nope
75. posted 11 Jul 2018, 21:44

2-1 Croatia Extra Time

Custerson
76. posted 14 Jul 2018, 11:44

Another Maternal DNA Match for hubby:-

Predicted relationship: 4th Cousins
Possible range: 4th - 6th cousins
Confidence: Good

DNA Match Custerson
4th cousin 2x removed
Father of DNA Match Custerson (1911 - 2002)

Ann Custerson (1878 - 1969)
Grandmother of DNA Match
Reuben Custerson (1847 - 1929)
father of Ann Custerson
Robert Custerson (1809 - 1884)
father of Reuben Custerson
Joseph Custerson (1770 - 1831)
father of Robert Custerson
Elizabeth Jane Custerton (1803 -)
daughter of Joseph Custerson
John Gouldthorp (1834 - 1921)
son of Elizabeth Jane Custerton
Jane Elizabeth Gouldthrop (1855 - 1939)
daughter of John Gouldthorp
Hilda Emma Backhouse (1889 - 1963)
daughter of Jane Elizabeth Gouldthrop
Thomas Charles Maddox (1921 - 1994)
son of Hilda Emma Backhouse

I had a message from someone who was asking about a Thomas Kaley. Can't say I can see the name in husbands' tree. This person has been a DNA Match to husband pretty much I think since the test was done but as so distant (and presumably Paternal side as I recognise No names in his tree) I have never contacted them

Predicted relationship: Distant Cousins
Possible range: 5th - 8th cousins
Confidence: Moderate

Would be interesting if I can work out how they are connected.

9th Cousin
77. posted 14 Jul 2018, 12:23

There were no new shared ancestor hints for me so I found a new match with a very large tree (41,094 people!) to see if I could work out the connection...

Predicted relationship: 4th Cousins
Possible range: 4th - 6th cousins
Confidence: Good

Shared - Clapson, James, Richardson, Smith

The Clapson line were in Sussex and I had two people she had. Strange then that a shared ancestor didn't come up. I had nothing on anything from Benjamin Clapson Jnr so that is all taken from the matches tree. (I could copy in the dates and names they have but I want to do that)

All I can say is we must be connected via another line as I have never seen a match with this bad a prediction - 4th Cousins? She is coming up as a 9th Cousin!!

DNA Match
9th cousin
Father of DNA Match
Eileen
mother of dna father
Annie Miller
mother of Eileen
Charles miller
father of Annie Miller
Adeline Clapson
mother of Charles miller
William Clapson
father of Adeline Clapson
John Clapson
father of William Clapson
John Clapson
father of John Clapson
Benjamin Clapson (1701 - 1769)
father of John Clapson
Benjamin Clapson (1671 - 1750)
father of Benjamin Clapson
Mary Clapson (1708 -)
daughter of Benjamin Clapson
62

John Hoad (1735 - 1824)
son of Mary Clapson
Thomas Hoad (1772 - 1838)
son of John Hoad
Sarah Hoad (1796 - 1838)
daughter of Thomas Hoad
Eleanor Barber (1825 - 1867)
daughter of Sarah Hoad
Mercy Carley (1854 - 1909)
daughter of Eleanor Barber
Mark Green (1875 - 1935)
son of Mercy Carley

Lowell
78. posted 14 Jul 2018, 17:22

Got some dates:-

Eileen Mary James (1915 - 1999)
mother of dna father Burke
Annie Louisa Miller (1889 - 1973)
mother of Eileen Mary James
Charles William Miller (1862 - 1940)
father of Annie Louisa Miller
Adeline Clapson (1826 - 1891)
mother of Charles William Miller
William Clapson (1801 - 1881)
father of Adeline Clapson
John Clapson (1775 -)
father of William Clapson
John Clapson (1740 -)
father of John Clapson

Charles and Annie Miller (nee Smith) emigrated from Hellingly to Lowell MA, c1911-1915. Their descendants all appear to have stayed in the area.

Bit about Lowell from Wikipedia here:-

Malthouse
79. posted 15 Jul 2018, 13:20

Here is another match that should have come up automatically rather than me doing it myself as we both had Stephen in our trees:-

Predicted relationship: Distant Cousins
Possible range: 5th - 8th cousins
Confidence: Moderate

DNA Match Charman
5th cousin 2x removed
Frederick Charman (1918 -)
father of DNA Match Charman
Mary Holman (1877 -)
Grandmother of DNA Match Charman
Sarah Malthouse (1851 -)
mother of Mary Holman
Charles Malthouse (1823 -)
father of Sarah Malthouse
Charles Malthouse (1780 -)
father of Charles Malthouse
William Malthouse (1746 -)
father of Charles Malthouse
Stephen Malthouse (1778 - 1838)
son of William Malthouse
Ellen Malthouse (1819 - 1906)
daughter of Stephen Malthouse
Mary Ann Stapleton (1842 - 1893)
daughter of Ellen Malthouse

Holiday
80. posted 15 Jul 2018, 19:24

William Malthouse and Ann Holiday had at least 8 children including Ann Holiday Malthouse. Ann was baptised in Horsham on the 27th October 1787. On the 24th October 1809, Ann married James Jenkins. Ann and James had 3 daughters between 1813 and 1822 before he died. I don't know when that was, but it was between 1822 and 1830.

Ann remarried on the 5th April 1830 in Bolney to Jesse Cheesman. Jesse was also a widower. He had previously been married to Anne Jenkins. Jesse and Anne Jenkins had a daughter, Elizabeth, in 1816. So, Anne Jenkins died between 1816 and 1830. Ann Holiday Malthouse and Jesse had a child of their own, David, in 1830.

Jenkins is a common name. I cannot locate their baptism docs, too many to choose from. But I like to think that James Jenkins and Anne Jenkins were siblings. This would mean that Elizabeth was a cousin and a stepsister to Jane, Maria and Mary. (Just half-sister to David still)

Hunnesett
81. posted 15 Jul 2018, 20:07

William Clapson and Sarah Hunnesett had at least 9 children between 1827 and 1840. The first four; Godfrey & Adeline (both c1827?), Carlton (1830) and Emily Caroline (1831) were all baptised together on the 13th March 1831. The rest of the children were baptised in their birth years.

Brain n Tucknott
82. posted 16 Jul 2018, 18:25

Amazon Prime has had a sale day. Ancestry DNA kits appeared to be quite cheap so asked my nephew if he was willing to spit and he is, so I ordered one.

After getting DNA confirmations of my trees on the Paterson, Green and Gardner lines, I am really looking forward to getting some new matches. Especially re Swan as that was the coolest direct ancestor and for Tucknott due to the fact that is a 'bastardry' line so only had a few clues to start with. After all of the Tucknott/Green connections I do hope that line is right!

Excited.

Imperial Tobacco
83. posted 16 Jul 2018, 19:32

Freda Marjorie Goodman was born in India on the 27th February 1907. She
was baptised on the 25th March 1907 at Jubbulpore, Bengal. On the 21st
February 1928, she married John Clifford Ryper (Roper?) in Barielly, Bengal.
I have not found anything else out about John. There are no records of any
children.

Henry Ernest Malthouse was born on the 6th November 1902 in Tunbridge
Wells/Tonbridge   (not   clear   which   one).   According   to
https://www.thegazette.co.uk/London/issue/35176/page/3113/data.pdf   he was
given an emergency commission to 2nd Lieutenant in the Indian Army on the
17th March 1941.

It can therefore be assumed that Henry met Freda in India during the war?
After the war he at least was living in Hastings.

In 1950, they travelled as a married couple on the boat Circassia from Bombay
to Liverpool. They arrived on the 19th June. On the 28th October, he
travelled back to India without Freda, again on the Circassia. At some point
he returned to England as he is living in Lewisham in 1951.

In 1954 he was in Australia. His occupation is given as a 'traffic manager' and
Freda does not appear to be with him. Henry arrived back in Southampton
on the 6th August on the ship Strathmore. On the 10th December, both
Henry and Freda are on the Canton, travelling to Bombay. They return on
the 20th March 1957 on the Circassia. Henry is now a Sales Manager.

At some point Henry and Freda go to Australia as they return on the 27th
April 1959 on the Stratheden. Henry is now a manager for Imperial Tobacco.

66

Henry died in Lewes in 1971. Freda died in 1993 in Spalding, Lincs. They do not appear to have had any children.

The lack of a wedding doc for Henry and Freda is most frustrating. I only have a public tree (though with a photo) of Freda to give me her surname. I don't normally type up the globetrotters of the 1950s but these two intrigued me.

Pettifer
84. posted 20 Jul 2018, 20:32

Looking at matches with Pettifer in their tree and found one where the Pettifer's came from Kilsby. Had to be a distant cousin surely? Yes - very! I had Richard Pettifer, my 8th Gt Grandfather in my tree. The addition of his son Stephen and Stephens descendants are all from the match. Going by number of hints to review, I think the match has photos. I think this is the first time a distant cousin has had a tree go far back enough to make a connection. The ancestry prediction was accurate.

Predicted relationship: Distant Cousins
Possible range: 5th - 8th cousins
Confidence: Moderate

DNA Match
7th cousin 2x removed
Father of DNA Match
Grandmother of DNA Match
Myrtle Pettifer
Great Grandmother of DNA Match
James Pettifer (1848 -)
Father of Myrtle Pettifer
William Pettifer (1809 -)
Father of James Pettifer
William Pettifer (1785 -)
Father of William Pettifer
Stephen Pettifer (1749 -)
Father of William Pettifer

Richard Pettifer (1695 -)
Father of Stephen Pettifer
Richard Pettifer (1736 -)
Son of Richard Pettifer
Richard Pettifer (1770 -)
Son of Richard Pettifer
James Pettifer (1794 - 1833)
Son of Richard Pettifer
Mary Pettifer (1816 -)
Daughter of James Pettifer
Ann Smith (1836 - 1897)
Daughter of Mary Pettifer
Thomas Nicholls (1860 - 1896)
Son of Ann Smith

U.S., American Civil War Regiments, 1861-1866
85. posted 20 Jul 2018, 21:57

THIS POST REMOVED AS BORING

This post was many pages about William Pettifer and his service in the civil war which can still be found on my blog. Not sure why I didn't just post a link like I normally do.

William Pettifer
86. posted 20 Jul 2018, 22:59

William Pettifer was baptised in Kilsby on the 3rd December 1809. At some point he emigrated to America. There is an older Will Pettifer that is a chemist that travels on the President, arriving in New York on the 31st March 1832. He marries Sarah Giles on the 16th December 1844 in Rock Island, Illinois. This is where he lives for the majority of his life. William and Sarah have at least 9 children between 1845 and 1864. William works as a 'coal digger' in 1860.

On the 10th June 1861, William enlisted in Company H, Illinois 19th Infantry Regiment. He would have been 52. I think this is very old to be a soldier. A

68

very detailed account of the part he played in the Civil War was on the previous post. Have never seen so much information on Ancestry before. His service ended on the 9th July 1864. In 1870 William is working as a 'teamster'. On the 17th July 1876 he started receiving an invalid pension.

On the 14th May 1891, William went into a home for disabled veterans in Leavenworth, Kansas. He had varicose veins on both legs apparently caused by the war. William is described as being 5ft 8" tall, with hazel eyes and grey hair. He is now a barber. Very varied occupations. He was discharged on the 23rd July 1891 and there is a comment on his card that says, 'This man received $36'.

It is not clear when William died. He doesn't appear on later census. Sarah does receive his pension when she is a widow. Sarah is still alive in 1909 and she is living in Washington but no idea what happened to her after that.

So not photo hints, loads of Civil War record hints. The DNA match does have a 10-page letter written in 1954 by a Maude Pettifer about William and Sarah. I wish there was a transcript. It is readable but it would be easier to see the faint 1950s curly writing printed rather than on a screen. Talking about eyesight, I now have driving glasses. I can still legally drive without them, but everything is so much clearer with them. Getting old and falling apart.

Seaford
87. posted 21 Jul 2018, 19:15

Tried searching by place instead of surnames. Obviously tried Seaford first and got 9 matches. 2 people known to me, one match already found, 3 people with locked trees, leaving 3 very distinct possibles. Done the easy one first and it is nice to have my 6th Gt Grandfather Stephen Green having a DNA verification. I had all of these people in my tree until the Grandmother already.

Predicted relationship: Distant Cousins
Possible range: 5th - 8th cousins
Confidence: Moderate

DNA Match
6th cousin 1x removed
Father of DNA Match
Ellen Holden (1890 -)
Grandmother of DNA Match
Elizabeth Howell (1869 -)
Mother of Ellen Holden
Judith Green (1837 - 1912)
Mother of Elizabeth Howell
Stephen Green (1795 - 1863)
Father of Judith Green
Henry (Harry) Green (1772 - 1846)
Father of Stephen Green
Stephen Green (1740 - 1809)
Father of Henry (Harry) Green
John Green (1763 -)
Son of Stephen Green
Jesse Green (1786 - 1873)
Son of John Green
George Green (1817 - 1886)
Son of Jesse Green

Fanny Mary Costick
88. posted 21 Jul 2018, 19:28

Lucky to already have Fanny in my tree. Just added on the match tree. The prediction in a bit out so I wonder if we are connected another way too? Another Green verified.

Predicted relationship: 4th Cousins
Possible range: 4th - 6th cousins
Confidence: Good

DNA Match Worby
6th cousin 2x removed
Father of DNA Match

Eva Nellie Brooks
Grandmother of DNA Match
Fanny Mary Cosstick (1844 -)
Mother of Eva Nellie Brooks
William Costick (1798 - 1874)
Father of Fanny Mary Cosstick
Mary Green (1767 - 1848)
Mother of William Costick
Henry Green (1736 -)
Father of Mary Green
John Green (1712 - 1770)
Father of Henry Green
Stephen Green (1740 - 1809)
Son of John Green
John Green (1763 -)
Son of Stephen Green
Jesse Green (1786 - 1873)
Son of John Green

Frost
89. posted 21 Jul 2018, 20:10

No, not Frost*. The 3rd match hasn't been successful so far.

Predicted relationship: Distant Cousins
Possible range: 5th - 8th cousins
Confidence: Moderate

Our common surnames are Clapson, Potter, Taylor and Wood. Lots of familiar locations but cannot find any immediate matches.   Clapson in Warbleton will take some investigating, rest I won't bother with.

Match Tree Mary Clapson B: 1724 in Warbleton, Sussex D: 1800
My Tree Mary Clapson B: 20 Jun 1708 in Warbleton, England

Match Tree 4 Potters from Worth 1687-1793
My Tree Barbara Potter

Match Tree John Taylor 1680 - 1721 Rotherfield & Elizabeth Taylor 1715 - 1797 Chiddingley Framfield
My Tree 6 Taylors from Brighton 1701-1872

Match Tree Ann Ward Wood B: 1672 in Heathfield, Sussex, D: Feb 1754 in Heathfield, Sussex
My Tree Hannah Wood B: abt 1706 in Lullington, Sussex & Susanna Wood B: 1708

However, I have found a nonblood connection to the DNA Match:-

DNA Match
5th great-nephew of wife of 5th great-uncle
Edith May Frost
Mother of DNA Match
Ernest Frost
Father of Edith May Frost
Henry Frost
Father of Ernest Frost
Mary Ann Cottington
Mother of Henry Frost
Charles Cottington (1807 -)
Father of Mary Ann Cottington
Charles Cottington (1776 -)
Father of Charles Cottington
James Cottington
Father of Charles Cottington
Jane Cottington (1778 - 1856)
Daughter of James Cottington
Charles Banks (1779 - 1857)
husband of Jane Cottington
John Banks (1754 - 1854)
Father of Charles Banks
Elizabeth Banks (1787 - 1866)
Daughter of John Banks
George Green (1817 - 1886)
Son of Elizabeth Banks
Albert Green (1853 - 1914)

Son of George Green

Obviously, there must be a real connection.

Radwinter
90. posted 21 Jul 2018, 21:05

Searched Radwinter on the boy -

Predicted relationship: Distant Cousins
Possible range: 5th - 8th cousins
Confidence: Moderate

DNA Match
4th cousin 1x removed of son
Eastgate
Mother of DNA Match
Walter Eastgate
Father of Eastgate
Harry Eastgate
Father of Walter Eastgate
Maria Andrews (1841 -)
Mother of Harry Eastgate
Thomas Andrews (1805 -)
Father of Maria Andrews
Josiah Andrews (1848 - 1898)
Son of Thomas Andrews
Elizabeth Andrews (1875 -)
Daughter of Josiah Andrews
Daisy Clark (1898 - 1958)
Daughter of Elizabeth Andrews
Robert William Gardner (1926 - 2000)
Son of Daisy Clark

East Hoathly
91. posted 22 Jul 2018, 10:14

This place search returns several knowns, a few locked, some that I keep seeing but can't work out the connection and one which had 3 shared surnames, 2 of which were irrelevant and one which was Pollard.

Their Pollards come from Pagham and Sidlesham. My Ann Pollard has been a brick wall. I know she married William Shelley on the 6th November 1778 in Rustington which is not too far away from Pagham.

They have parents of Richard Pollard (born c 1791) being Thomas and Ann. I have a 'potential' hint of Ann's parents being Thomas and Ann too.

Thomas Pollard and Ann Shepherd married in Arundel on the 29th July 1760. If Ann was their born later that year it would make her only 18 when she married William.

Family Search returns only one person born in Pagham between 1760 and 1780 with parents Thomas and Ann - Joyce. It returns 7 with those parameters in West Hoathly which is a long way away. A Richard Pollard was born in 1760 in Fletching, but parents are called Richard and Sarah. There are 3 Ann Pollards born but I think it is 1762 with Thomas and Ann in West Hoathly - not sure why it didn't come up when searched the other way. If it is though, she would only be 16 when she married William.

As much as I would like to make some sort of connection between me and this match, too many unproven assumptions to say Richard and Ann are siblings.

Ethnicity Update
92. posted 22 Jul 2018, 12:50

I got bored doing random searches on places and names, so thought I would refresh ethnicity. IT WAS A MAJOR REFRESH. Low confidence regions have been eliminated and the existing regions are more specific. Husband is now 100% English. I am not a Viking anymore - that bit is now Swedish. I am not at risk of being French anymore as that bit is now German. (yay!)

74

Biggest change is for the boy who previously was not considered British but is now 87% English. How mad.

Mary Clapson
93. posted 22 Jul 2018, 20:53

"I had nothing on anything from Benjamin Clapson Jnr so that is all taken from the matches tree." They have Benjamin Clapson (1701) as marrying Martha and they have a son called John in 1740.

From looking at the Frost/Clapson connection, they say Benjamin married Jane and they have a daughter called Mary in 1724.

(It has taken me an unnecessarily long time to work out the connection between their Mary Clapson (1724) and my Mary Clapson (1708), both born Warbleton because of his wife being Martha and not Jane)

Who to believe? Maybe they are both wrong? Maybe they are both right? (Jane could have died and he then he remarried to Martha.)

Assuming they are both right, the match that was previously by coincidence my 5th great-nephew of wife of 5th great-uncle, is now:-

DNA Match
8th cousin 1x removed
Edith Frost
Mother of DNA Match
Ernest Frost
Father of Edith Frost
Henry (Harry) Frost
Father of Ernest Frost
William Frost
Father of Henry (Harry) Frost
William Frost
Father of William Frost
Sarah Ann Cornford
Mother of William Frost

Mary Clapson (1724 -)
Mother of Sarah Ann Cornford
Benjamin Clapson (1701 - 1769)
Father of Mary Clapson
Benjamin Clapson (1671 - 1750)
Father of Benjamin Clapson
Mary Clapson (1708 -)
Daughter of Benjamin Clapson
John Hoad (1735 - 1824)
Son of Mary Clapson
Thomas Hoad (1772 - 1838)
Son of John Hoad
Sarah Hoad (1796 - 1838)
Daughter of Thomas Hoad
Eleanor Barber (1825 - 1867)
Daughter of Sarah Hoad
Mercy Carley (1854 - 1909)

Scorchio
94. posted 26 Jul 2018, 01:12

It's been around 5 years since I last mentioned 1976.
https://sites.google.com/site/theashleaze/genealogy/research-blog/wolverine

That was nothing like it is at the moment. Never known anything like it, can't remember when it last rained. Apparently it is the driest it has been since 1961 but still not 1976.

"...but 1976 was in a different league to this year. It saw an extraordinary 18 days running when somewhere in the UK had temperatures above 30C.
The latest figures for 2018 show that, so far, we've had "only" nine days on the trot above 30C. Also, 1976 had a staggering 15 consecutive days in which temperatures topped 32C"

https://www.bbc.co.uk/news/uk-44943672

10 degrees

95. posted 28 Jul 2018, 16:17

Yesterday at precisely the forecast time, there was an all too brief thunderstorm. Of course I was in it and got saturated. It didn't seem to help though. Today - hurray! - only 23 degrees and it is windy. Feels SOOOOOOOOOOOOOOOOO nice being 10 degrees cooler than it has been in an age. Back in the 30s again next week though :(

In other news, saw nephew today and collected his spit. That has been duly posted, though next collection isn't until Monday.

Just the waiting now...

Secrist
96. posted 29 Jul 2018, 17:29

I have been putting 'dna match' profile pics on my matches and did the Barber related ones last. Have actually looked at some of the hints. Turns out Henry Barbers wifes surnames is Geall. She must be his cousin and therefore a cousin of mine too. However, her father is called Jasper born c1802 and I cannot find his birth parent names to establish a connection.

Henry Barber and his sister Hannah Barber and their spouses, Martha Geall and John Edward Ellis are in the 'Conquerors of the West: Stalwart Mormon Pioneers, Vols. 1-2'.

This database is a collection of histories compiled by The National Society of the Sons of the Utah Pioneers. This database includes the first two volumes produced by The Sons of the Utah Pioneers and indexes persons with the last names A-L. The database includes names, dates, and other vital information about the lives of Mormon (The Church of Jesus Christ of Latter-day Saints) pioneers who settled in Utah.

The records were compiled using information that was sent to The Sons of the Utah Pioneers. The following statement appears in the introduction to the volumes, "I have only the record and information that was sent to me. If, in reading this record you find an error, I hope you will recognize that when we deal with old records, we must accept that there will undoubtedly be errors or differences of opinion. I only had someone's word that it was right. It would have been impossible for me to research every entry."

I then found a new shared ancestor hint; the DNA Match was already in my tree as she appears in the 1940 US Census. Bit weird to think of people being alive but showing up on a census doc. Quite inaccurate prediction.

Predicted relationship: Distant Cousins
Possible range: 5th - 8th cousins
Confidence: Moderate

DNA Match
3rd cousin 2x removed
Father of DNA Match (1909 - 1994)
Father of DNA Match
Ruth Barber (1874 - 1939)
Grandmother of DNA Match
David Barber (1833 - 1912)
Father of Ruth Barber
Thomas Barber (1793 - 1862)
Father of David Barber
Eleanor Barber (1825 - 1867)
Daughter of Thomas Barber

French
97. posted 29 Jul 2018, 19:16

John French was born c1806 in Chiddlingley and he married Phyllis c1828. They went on to have at least 10 children between 1828 and 1852. Phyllis must have died in the 1850s as by 1861, John is a widow. Two of their children were Sarah born in 1832 and Esther born in 1852. John died in 1862.

David Barber was born on the 5th September 1833. He was one of the children of Thomas Barber and Sarah Hoad. In 1855, David married Sarah French. They had at least 8 children between 1851 (!) and 1874. In 1861, he also had his father in law, John French, and two of his children, George and

Esther living with him. In 1871, Esther is the only in law living with them.
The Barber family had moved from Chiddingley to Pembroke, Kent by this
time. On the 15th September 1875, Sarah died in a lunatics' asylum in
Tonbridge.

David took his family and Esther to America. They left Liverpool on the
Wyoming, arriving in New York on the 23rd June 1877. Whereas in England
his occupation is an Ag Lab, in the US he is a farmer. They are living in
Centreville, Davis, Utah in 1880. On the 1880 census Esther is listed as his
spouse rather than his sister-in-law. David and Esther had at least 4 children
between 1878 and 1883 when Esther dies. David remains in Centreville until
his death on the 22nd April 1912.

My suspicious mind thinks that 6 children were David and Sarah's and that 6
children were David and Esther's. The last two were born between the 1871
census and Sarah's death in the asylum. It all depends on when she went into
the asylum. And did David put her there to be with Esther? You can imagine
them plotting their new life in America, they certainly went very soon after
Sarah's death.

Thomas Barber
98. posted 29 Jul 2018, 23:39

Here's a way to waste several hours of a Sunday evening and miss Poldark*...
The latest DNA match was the 7th that was descendant from Thomas or 6th
if you disregard the son who also had a test. The only one of these coming
up as a Utah Pioneer is Hannah Barber and as far as I can tell she didn't even
get there, she died in Greenriver, Sweetwater, Wyoming, just 3 months after
arriving in New York. I guess it is due to her husband. I digress. I have
drawn up a little tree showing our connections:-

I wonder how many more I will get?

*no such thing as missing a programme of course but this is one I generally watch live,
along with the fantastic Versailles on Monday nights, shall miss them both when the series
finish

Vilate
99.   posted 1 Aug 2018, 21:55

Whilst I wait for the results to come back, I am going through Barber descendants. Not something I have ever bothered with before due to the fact these trees are heavily documented already. Things I have noticed. 1) They seem to be born in Utah, get married in Idaho and die in Utah. What's that all about? 2) Whereas I might get 3 or 4 hints on a date, there are about 7 or 8 and finally 3) of these documents, the dates don't match. They will be out by a day or the day and month will match but the year will be out by 1 or 2 years. And this is with EVERY person and there are a LOT of people. They really can chuck out babies. But if they want to save their ancestors they need to get their facts straight.

Also, no weird multi marriages. Though they do get married and remarried and sometimes remarried again. (The spouses do appear to have died.)

I have a few run of the mill marriages to type up but can't be bothered tonight. One of them is where David Moroni Scott marries his stepsister. So, we have either:-

> Marinda Vilate Hargraves (1892 - 1976)
> **stepdaughter of husband of 1st cousin 4x removed**
> Marinda Vilate Weaver (1864 - 1945)
> Mother of Marinda Vilate Hargraves
> John William Scott (1844 - 1916)
> husband of Marinda Vilate Weaver
> Fanny Mariah Ellis (1849 - 1894)
> wife of John William Scott
> Hannah Barber (1821 - 1864)
> Mother of Fanny Mariah Ellis
> **Thomas Barber (1793 - 1862)**
> Father of Hannah Barber

> or

> Marinda Vilate Hargraves (1892 - 1976)

80

wife of 2nd cousin 3x removed
David Moroni Scott (1884 - 1968)
husband of Marinda Vilate Hargraves
Fanny Mariah Ellis (1849 - 1894)
Mother of David Moroni Scott

Sweden
100.posted 2 Aug 2018, 20:28

Fanny Mariah Ellis was born in 1849 in Sussex, her parents were John Edward Ellis and Hannah Barber. When she was 14, she emigrated with her family on the Hudson, arriving in New York on the 20th July 1864.

(Note for Utah posts I do not know what dates are right. I just pick one of the two or three that is hinted.)

Fanny married John William Scott on the 11th January 1874 at Endowment House, Salt Lake City. I think this is her LDS baptism date too.

Fanny and John had at least 6 children including David Moroni Scott before she died on the 7th February 1894, aged just 44. John remarried on the 31st March 1897 in Logan. Cache, Utah. His new wife, Marinda Vilate Weaver, had also been married before. She was previously married to Alexander Samuel Hargreaves and they had at least 4 children including Marinda Vilate Hargreaves. Alexander died in 1893, aged just 33. A story on Ancestry says that whilst climbing he stepped on his gun, making it go off and shot himself by accident.

John and Marinda went on to have at least 4 children of their own. By 1910 they had moved to Bingham, Idaho where John died on the 16th October 1916 and Marinda died on the 16th June 1945.

As is known from the previous post, David Moroni Scott married Marinda Vilate Hargreaves. This was on the 29th October 1917 in Bannock, Idaho. They had been living together already for past 20 years. They are not related. They are step step siblings.

The other four sons of Fanny and John also have interesting marriages.

Gottfried Malmberg aka Godfried Malm and his wife Selma were born in Sweden and emigrated to America c1886. They had several children in both Sweden and America including Hazel Malm and Esther Malm.

Arthur Leroy Scott married Esther on the 20th December 1911. Harold Sylvester Scott married Hazel on the 13th March 1912.

Ola Olson and his wife Ellen Elna Jensen (? - not sure of her name) were both born in Sweden too. They arrived in 1866, 20 years before the Malms. As such they get on the pioneer list. Ola and Ellen have several children including Hilma Ellen Olson and Olive Olson.

Ernest Royal Scott married Olive on the 21st March 1900. John William Edward Scott married Hilma on the 11th February 1903.

Wooler
101.posted 3 Aug 2018, 21:18

New match for me. I had John Geal in my tree, Lucy Geal and her descendants are new. All stayed in Sussex area.

Predicted relationship: Distant Cousins
Possible range: 5th - 8th cousins
Confidence: Moderate

DNA Match
7th cousin
Mother of DNA Match
Gwendoline Cecila Wooler (1909 -)
Grand Mother of DNA Match
Horace Wooler (1853 -)
Father of Gwendoline Cecila Wooler
Jabez Wooler
Father of Horace Wooler
William Wooler (1816 -)

Father of Jabez Wooller
Lucy Geal (1784 -)
Mother of William Wooller
John Geal (1757 - 1844)
Father of Lucy Geal
Thomas Geall (1735 -)
Father of John Geal
Ann Geall (1765 - 1845)
Daughter of Thomas Geall
Thomas Barber (1793 - 1862)
Son of Ann Geall

Camelot
102. posted 3 Aug 2018, 21:29

John Thomas Barker and Annetta Andrus had a daughter called Genevieve Barker. John had a brother called Ernest. Ernest and Sarah Amy Blodgett had a son called Merlin Barker.

Genevieve and Merlin are cousins!

Missionary
103.posted 4 Aug 2018, 09:13

Ellen Louisa Wooller is one of the children of Jabez Wooler and Elizabeth Trehern Relf. She was born in Preston, Sussex in 1894. On the 19th December 1919, she went to Bombay, India. Her occupation is given as missionary. Ellen went to India again on the 26th October 1926. She travelled to Japan at some point, arriving back in the UK on the 19th August 1932. Ellen went back to India on the 12th January 1934. Ellen died in Kasur, Lahore, India at the Zenana Bible and Medical Mission Bungalow on the 16th February 1944. She left £497 19s to Katharine Norman, her older sister.

Zenana Missions (from wiki)

Different times. This photo sums it up (from a public tree on Ancestry):-

Bennion
104.posted 4 Aug 2018, 13:06

This is a match to daughter but bizarrely not a match to her father. But then he has a couple that she doesn't have. Weird. Anyway, not sure of this because I only had Henry Martin in my tree. The daughter of Henry is apparently born in South Africa and then marries someone who may or may not have been born in England or Africa and then they move to Florida. I don't like not having any sort of documentation to back up a connection. Their tree maybe wrong after all. In addition, the shared ancestor hint has the match as 5th Cousin 1x removed and I can't work out where I am missing a generation. Meh.

Assuming their tree is correct....

Predicted relationship: Distant Cousins
Possible range: 5th - 8th cousins
Confidence: Moderate

DNA Match
5th cousin (therefore 4th Cousin 1x removed of husband)
Father of DNA Match
Mary Bell Ricketts (1912 -)
Grandmother of DNA Match
Annie Winifred Bennion (1883 -)
Mother of Mary Bell Ricketts
Susan Martin (1863 -)
Mother of Annie Winifred Bennion
Henry Martin (1832 -)
Father of Susan Martin
Richard Martin (1796 -)
Father of Henry Martin
Sarah Martin (1830 - 1916)
Daughter of Richard Martin
Eliza Martin (1848 - 1911)
Daughter of Sarah Martin
Thomas Henry Maddox (1887 - 1981)
Son of Eliza Martin

Ann Nichols
105.posted 4 Aug 2018, 13:41

Really could not find anything on Henry Martin. The only evidence of his wife was a wedding doc in London with a name of Henry Richard Martin. So, I thought, lets just save it anyway and see what happens. It came up with 'this is saved to Ann Nichols in the Paterson/Green tree'.

Which would explain why her father isn't a match but then surely, I should be one instead? Had a look at the DNA matches tree and yep - it is my Ann Nichols:-

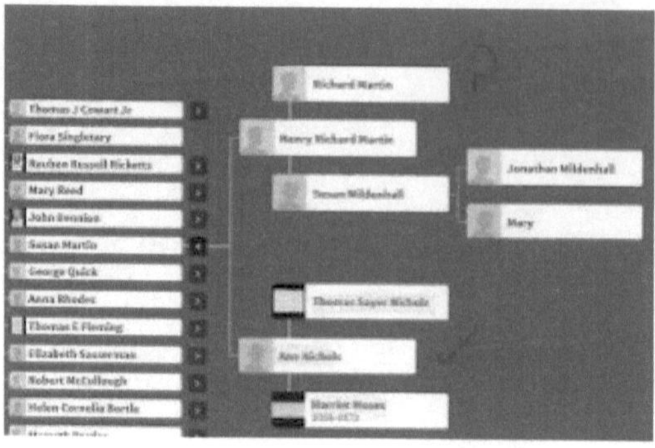

So, if my Ann Nichols married Henry Martin, it means that the Paterson/Green and Ashley trees are connected.

Nicholls
106.posted 4 Aug 2018, 14:19

Currently I have confirmation of a connection on my line through Thomas Sayer Nicholls, making me a 5th cousin:-

DNA Match
5th cousin
Father of DNA Match
Mary Bell Ricketts
Grandmother of DNA Match
Annie Winifred Bennion
Mother of Mary Bell Ricketts
Susan Martin
Mother of Annie Winifred Bennion
Ann Nichols (1828 -)
Mother of Susan Martin
Thomas Sayer Nicholls (1803 - 1853)
Father of Ann Nichols
James Nicholls (1832 - 1872)
Son of Thomas Sayer Nicholls
Thomas Nicholls (1860 - 1896)
Son of James Nicholls

86

Florence Catherine M Nicholls (1893 - 1927)
Daughter of Thomas Nicholls

I have a theory that these matches are so weak that they don't show up for husband and I. But cos daughter has matches in both lines it doubles up the DNA strength of the Martins/Nicholls giving a shared match. Here was the original hint and then there is a potential confirming all of this.

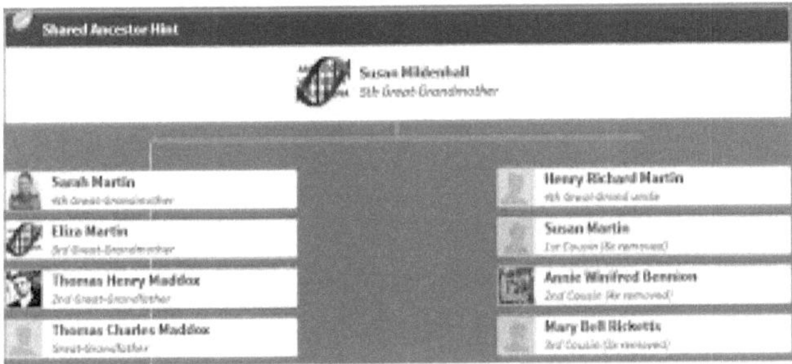

Presently I only have evidence of a Richard Martin and a Susannah. Probably safe to say Susannah is Susan Mildenhall.

Maddox Green Connection
107.posted 4 Aug 2018, 15:03

Husband
4th great-nephew of husband of 4th great-aunt
Thomas Charles Maddox
Grandfather of Husband
Thomas Henry Maddox
Father of Thomas Charles Maddox
Eliza Martin
Mother of Thomas Henry Maddox
Sarah Martin
Mother of Eliza Martin

Richard Martin
Father of Sarah Martin
Henry Richard Martin (1833 -)
Son of Richard Martin
Ann Nichols (1828 -)
wife of Henry Richard Martin
Thomas Sayer Nicholls (1803 - 1853)
Father of Ann Nichols

I see little point filling in the dates etc.

Barber Take2
108. posted 4 Aug 2018, 23:58

Missed a Barber match. I wish I stuck to a font style & size as have no idea what I used. The father of Bonnie Ellis is not connected to my Ellis surprisingly.

Rain
109.posted 9 Aug 2018, 21:23

Today has been the first day it has rained all day. The temperature is so much better. Now there is thunder rumbling. Just in time for my holiday to Cornwall.

Nephew test is already at analyzing stage, results no doubt will arrive when I am in Cornwall in the rain.

Charles Barber was born in Chiddingley on the 30th January 1863. He arrived in New York on the 5th June 1878. Charles married Alice Evelyn Kent in 1887 and they had at least 5 children including Alice Erma Barber. Alice died in 1930. Charles remarried on the 12th May 1931 to Esther Bates, previously Sessions, nee Tolman. Charles died in 1933.

Esther Tolman and her first husband Percy Sessions had at least 4 children including Oel Clark Sessions. Oel married his stepsister Alice Barber on the 18th December 1912.

Negus
110.posted 18 Aug 2018, 20:05

It was cold but mostly dry this week in Cornwall. Glad I took the wetsuit!

As expected, results are in. Reckon 5 matches to look at, quite pleased about that. Husband and I also have a new match each. His first:-

Predicted relationship: Distant Cousins
Possible range: 5th - 8th cousins
Confidence: Good

DNA Match
4th cousin 1x removed
Mother of DNA Match
Charlotte Negus (1874 -)
Grandmother of DNA Match
Ellis Negus (1842 -)
Father of Charlotte Negus
Mary Ann Stafford (1823 -)
Mother of Ellis Negus
John Stafford (1800 -)
Father of Mary Ann Stafford
Emma Stafford (1836 -)
Daughter of John Stafford
Jane Elizabeth Gouldthrop (1855 - 1939)
Daughter of Emma Stafford
Hilda Emma Backhouse (1889 - 1963)
Daughter of Jane Elizabeth Gouldthrop

Sadly, another for his maternal line. One day I will get a paternal clue. Mary Ann Stafford and descendants are all new. Loads of hints to look at, just adding her enabled me to get to my match without even looking at his tree.

Tucknott
111.posted 18 Aug 2018, 20:50

My new match was my nephew - duh!!

First up, confirmation of his Mums paternal line. Problem being that this line
connects with our Green line, so it comes up with a stupid relationship:- 1st
cousin 3x removed of husband of 1st cousin 6x removed.

Anyway:-

Predicted relationship: 4th Cousins
Possible range: 4th - 6th cousins
Confidence: High

DNA Match
3rd Cousin 2x removed
Edward Henry Forrest (1915 - 1988)
Father of DNA Match
Mary Ann Tucknott (1876 - 1943)
Mother of Edward Henry Forrest
James Tucknott (1844 - 1886)
Father of Mary Ann Tucknott
George Tucknott (1799 - 1876)
Father of John Tucknott (1826-1908)
John Tucknott (1864-1949)
Father of Albert Edward Tucknott (1900-1961)
Great Grandfather of Nephew

Mary Ann Tucknott and descendants are new. Had James in 1871 and the
family disappears. Mary being born in 1876 was too late for that census.

To Do
112.posted 18 Aug 2018, 21:51

Done a couple more Tucknott matches:-

Tucknott 2
Predicted relationship: 4th Cousins
90

Possible range: 4th - 6th cousins
Confidence: Good

DNA match
1st cousin 4x removed of husband of 1st cousin 6x removed
3rd Cousin 1x removed

Tucknott 3
Predicted relationship: 4th Cousins
Possible range: 4th - 6th cousins
Confidence: Good

DNA Match
1st cousin 5x removed of husband of 1st cousin 6x removed
5th Cousin

Then I went through the 31 matches to see if any were not Tucknott. Ignoring the 2 locked and the ones I already have in my own matches, there are 13 to check out:-

2 locked
2 Saddletons
(Nicholls to check)
4 Barbers I don't have?
Steer (Tucknott)
Smith (Tucknott)
William Tucknott (6th!!)
Wraight (Saddleton)
Richard Robinson - I don't have?
The OTHER Barber line - I don't have?

I will ignore the Barbers for now but very interested in the non-Mormon Barber line so will check that out. Also there seems to be another Thomas Sayer Nicholls connection that needs looking into.

Swain
113.posted 18 Aug 2018, 22:26

This is a new connection for me, strange how I only know about it from the Nephews tree:-

Predicted relationship to Nephew: Distant Cousins
Possible range: 5th - 8th cousins
Confidence: Moderate

DNA Match
5th cousin
Hazel LaJune Hansen (1925 - 1984)
Mother of DNA
Winifred Meakin (1897 - 1972)
Mother of Hazel LaJune Hansen
Edward Meakin (1867 - 1906)
Father of Winifred Meakin
Harriet Swain (1827 -)
Mother of Edward Meakin
Mary Barber (1803 -)
Mother of Harriet Swain
John Barber (1778 - 1861)
Father of Mary Barber
Ann Barber (1800 - 1888)
Daughter of John Barber
Frances Pell (1843 - 1924)
Daughter of Ann Barber
Hannah Turfitt (1879 - 1950)
Daughter of Frances Pell

Harriet Swain was in my tree but hadn't looked at her hints prior to this evening so all her descendants are new. This is my Pell Barber line, not my Carley Barber line. However, guess where she and her husband Samuel Meakin appear to have ended up... Utah.

92

Barnsby
114.posted 19 Aug 2018, 00:24

Another clue came whilst I was on holiday. Before I went my son had a match to a locked tree and so I sent them a message and also lists of possible surnames that could be a match and it turns out they are a descendant of Grace Barnsby that I already had in my tree:-

Predicted relationship: 4th Cousins
Possible range: 4th - 6th cousins
Confidence: Good

DNA Match
2nd cousin 2x removed of son
Grace Barnsby (1879 -)
Grandmother of DNA Match
John Barnsby (1827 - 1902)
Father of Grace Barnsby
Susan Maria Barnsby (1861 - 1940)
Daughter of John Barnsby
Joseph Edwin Fearn (1897 - 1983)
Son of Susan Maria Barnsby
Doreen Joan Fearn (1929 - 1985)

Crosby
115.posted 19 Aug 2018, 11:59

The Robinson match was new and Jane Robinson and her descendants new to my tree:-

Predicted relationship: Distant Cousins
Possible range: 5th - 8th cousins
Confidence: Moderate

DNA Match
6th cousin

Kenneth Crosby
Grandfather of DNA Match
Richard Crosby
Father of Kenneth Crosby
Richard Robinson Crosby (1880 -)
Father of Richard Crosby
Stephen Crosby (1845 -)
Father of Richard Robinson Crosby
Jane Robinson (1812 -)
Mother of Stephen Crosby
Richard Robinson (1769 - 1836)
Father of Jane Robinson
George Robinson (1794 - 1824)
Son of Richard Robinson
Trueman Robinson (1817 - 1891)
Son of George Robinson

Saddleton
116.posted 19 Aug 2018, 12:11

Predicted relationship: Distant Cousins
Possible range: 5th - 8th cousins
Confidence: Moderate

DNA Match
3rd cousin 3x removed of nephew
Robert Henry Saddleton (1911 -)
Father of DNA Match
Herbert John Saddleton (1862 - 1943)
Father of Robert Henry Saddleton
Henry Saddleton (1838 - 1924)
Father of Herbert John Saddleton
John Saddleton (1790 - 1870)
Father of Henry Saddleton
George Saddleton (1811 - 1899)
Son of John Saddleton

John Robert Saddleton (1856 - 1915)
Son of George Saddleton
George G Saddleton (1900 -)
Son of John Robert Saddleton
Evelyn Maude Violet Saddleton (1920 - 1994)
Daughter of George G Saddleton

Predicted relationship: Distant Cousins
Possible range: 5th - 8th cousins
Confidence: Moderate

DNA Match
3rd cousin 1x removed of nephew
Eric V Jordan (1913 - 1978)
Grandfather of DNA Match
Marguerite Eliza Mary Saddleton (1884 - 1960)
Mother of Eric V Jordan
John Robert Saddleton (1856 - 1915)
Father of Marguerite Eliza Mary Saddleton
George G Saddleton (1900 -)
Son of John Robert Saddleton

The next Saddleton match is all new from Hannah Wraight:-

Predicted relationship: Distant Cousins
Possible range: 5th - 8th cousins
Confidence: Moderate

DNA Match
6th cousin 2x removed of nephew
Daisy Maytum
Grandmother of DNA Match
Ellen Butcher
Mother of Daisy Maytum
John Butcher
Father of Ellen Butcher
Hannah Wraight
Mother of John Butcher
William Wraight (1756 -)

Father of Hannah Wraight
William Wraight (1725 - 1791)
Father of William Wraight
James Wraight (1759 - 1853)
Son of William Wraight
Celia Wraight (1791 - 1867)
Daughter of James Wraight
George Saddleton (1811 - 1899)
Son of Celia Wraight

Barber 9
117.posted 19 Aug 2018, 14:51

Predicted relationship: Distant Cousins
Possible range: 5th - 8th cousins
Confidence: Moderate

DNA Match
3rd cousin 2x removed
Horace David Barber (1861 - 1924)
Grandfather of DNA Match
David Barber (1833 - 1912)
Father of Horace David Barber
Thomas Barber (1793 - 1862)
Father of David Barber

Tripe Dresser
118.posted 19 Aug 2018, 17:11

George Steer was born in Westerham c1848. I cannot find any birth docs for him. There is a hint giving a Richard and Sarah Steer baptising a son in 1849 in Westerham. In 1851, when he was 3, he lived with his grandparents, Israel and Frances Steer in Westerham. In 1861, he lived with his Aunt, Alice Tickell nee Steer. The Tickell family lived in Stepney. William Tickell was a pork butcher. George was still living with the Tickells in 1871 and he is working as a tripe dresser.

On the 12th July 1873, George marries Julia Emma Clark at St Mary's in Lambeth. He gives his father as Israel Steer. Julia dies in 1875.

On the 2nd June 1877, George marries Frances Eliza Mason at St Stephens in Walworth. Again, he gives his father as Israel Steer. It has to be assumed that he is giving his grandfather's name rather than his father's name. Israel Steer does not appear to have had a son called Israel. Israel Steer doesn't seem to have a son called Richard either.

In 1881 George and Frances are living in Bermondsey and he is now an unemployed tripe dresser. By 1891 he is back in the tripe dressing game as a foreman and in 1901 a manager. George and Frances had 9 children. They moved to Croydon by 1911. George died in Croydon in 1920.

The public trees give his mother as Caroline Steer who was a daughter of Israel Steer. She would have been 23 when George was born. In 1851, when George is living with her father Israel, she is in service in Camberwell. Caroline married Edward Capelin on the 1st August 1858 and they were living in Bermondsey with their own children whilst George was living with her sister Alice. Assuming the public trees are correct with her being Georges mother:-

Predicted relationship: Distant Cousins
Possible range: 5th - 8th cousins
Confidence: Moderate

DNA Match
5th cousin 1x removed of nephew
Doris Lilian Alderson (1907 -)
Grandmother of DNA Match
Lilian Steer (1878 -)
Mother of Doris Lilian Alderson
George Steer (1848 -1920)
Father of Lilian Steer
Caroline Steer (1825 -) or Israel or Richard or unknown
Mother of George Steer
Israel Steer (1783 - 1864)
Father of Caroline Steer

Mary Ann Steer (1810 - 1876)
Daughter of Israel Steer
Eliza Smith (1831 - 1901)
Daughter of Mary Ann Steer
John Tucknott (1864 - 1949)
Son of Eliza Smith

Barber 10 & 11
119.posted 19 Aug 2018, 18:07

Really one more

Predicted relationship: Distant Cousins
Possible range: 5th - 8th cousins
Confidence: Moderate

DNA Match
4th cousin 1x removed
Leda Asenith Ellis (1904 -)
Grandmother of DNA match
Thomas Henry Ellis (1851 - 1933)
Father of Leda Asenith Ellis
Hannah Barber (1821 - 1864)
Mother of Thomas Henry Ellis
Thomas Barber (1793 - 1862)
Father of Hannah Barber

DNA Match
5th cousin
Leda Asenith Ellis (1904 -)
Gt Grandmother DNA Match
Thomas Henry Ellis (1851 - 1933)
Father of Leda Asenith Ellis
Hannah Barber (1821 - 1864)

Barber 12
120.posted 19 Aug 2018, 18:54

Predicted relationship: Distant Cousins
Possible range: 5th - 8th cousins
Confidence: Moderate

DNA Match
3rd cousin 2x removed
Harry Barber (1868 - 1944)
Grandfather of DNA Match
Henry Barber (1827 - 1878)
Father of Harry Barber
Thomas Barber (1793 - 1862)
Father of Henry Barber

Barber 13
121.posted 19 Aug 2018, 19:39

Two of the hints make no sense so all hints are done now. Any new ones are now found by doing it myself. Bored so bored of Barber.

Predicted relationship: 4th Cousins
Possible range: 4th - 6th cousins
Confidence: High

DNA match
4th cousin 1x removed
Sarah Grace Barber (1883 - 1966)
Grandmother of DNA match
Julia B Barber (1860 - 1951)
Mother of Sarah Grace Barber
Benjamin Barber (1828 - 1899)
Father of Julia B Barber
Thomas Barber (1793 - 1862)
Father of Benjamin Barber

Eliza Martin
122.posted 20 Aug 2018, 21:13

A close match for Martin in Lambeth came up and thought it warranted investigation. They had very similar names in their tree:-

Predicted relationship: 4th Cousins
Possible range: 4th - 6th cousins
Confidence: Very High

Me:-
Charles Martin c1815 Lambeth
Alfred Frederick John Martin 1853 Lambeth

Match:-
Henry Charles Martin c1815 Lambeth
Alfred Martin 1853 Lambeth

Turns out I already had Henry Charles Martin in my tree, but I had disconnected him from Alfred Frederick John Martin. I have reconnected them. Which means:-

DNA Match
3rd cousin 1x removed of nephew
Edwin Inwood Roberts (1874 -)
Grandfather of DNA Match
Eliza Martin (1842 -)
Mother of Edwin Inwood Roberts
Henry Charles Martin (1816 -)
Father of Eliza Martin
Alfred Frederick John Martin (1853 - 1932)
Son of Henry Charles Martin
Florence Louise Martin (1895 - 1970)
Daughter of Alfred Frederick John Martin
Albert Alfred Tucknott (1924 - 1973)
Son of Florence Louise Martin

This was a very useful match as it confirmed that Henry Charles Martin and Charles Martin are the same person. Looking at the documentation, I am not sure why I ever thought it was not the case.

Arnold Costin
123.posted 20 Aug 2018, 23:29

Arnold Costin was baptised at St Mary's in Lewisham on the 13th October 1816. In 1841 he was working as an ag lab and was boarding with his younger siblings. In 1846 he married Elizabeth Tucknott in West Wickham. Arnold and Elizabeth went on to have at least 6 children. In 1851, the family are still in West Wickham and he is still an ag lab.

On the 12th March 1855, Arnold was on trial at Maidstone Court for attempted suicide. He appears to have been discharged. It seems incomprehensible that someone who tried to commit suicide and failed would then be arrested and possibly imprisoned. It was still illegal in the UK up to 1961!

In 1861, the family were living in Deptford and Arnold is now a stoker on the railways though I have not found an employment records to confirm this.

In 1870, Arnold and his family emigrated to Australia on the Indus. They arrived at Moreton Bay on the 21st July 1870. Arnold died on the 1st October 1886 in Brisbane.

Fressingfield
124.posted 22 Sep 2018, 09:57

My 6th cousin 1x removed on the Green line sent me a message that my nephew was coming up as a dna match to her husband when she entered the name Pelling. At first, I thought it was a connection via the Tucknotts but that didn't make sense as they are in her line (marrying the Greens) rather than her husbands.

So, I looked at the surnames and locations of her husband's lines that matched with my nephews line and my guess is that the DNA link comes from his Suffolk Barber line but cannot make an official connection. Her husband has a Mary Barber born c1751 in Fressingfield and nephew has John Barber born c1784 in Syleham.

Syleham is only 4 miles away from Fressingfield.

Therefore it is a possibility that her husband is also my nephews 5th cousin 2x removed:-

Husband of my 6th Cousin 1x removed
5th cousin 2x removed of nephew
Stephen Charles Allen (1890 -)
Father of Husband of my 6th Cousin 1x removed
Julia Lincoln (1860 -)
Mother of Stephen Charles Allen
Elizabeth Clutton (1815 -)
Mother of Julia Lincoln
John Clutton (1780 -)
Father of Elizabeth Clutton
Mary Barber (1745 -)
Mother of John Clutton
Barber (1720 -)
Father of Mary Barber
Barber (1760 -)
Son of Barber
John Barber (1784 -)
Son of Barber
John Barber (1822 -)
Son of John Barber
Julia Barber (1854 -)
Daughter of John Barber
Florence Louise Martin (1895 - 1970)
Daughter of Julia Barber
Albert Alfred Tucknott (1924 - 1973)
Son of Florence Louise Martin

The italics is the guess. Mary Barber and her descendants copied from my cousins tree.

"In 1870-72, John Marius Wilson's Imperial Gazetteer of England and Wales described Syleham like this:

SYLEHAM, a parish in Hoxne district, Suffolk; on the river Waveney, 3½ miles SW of Harleston r. station. Post town, Scole. Acres, 1,603. Real property, £2,967. Pop., 357. Houses, 64. The property is subdivided. S. Hall is the seat of the Rev. A. Cooper. There is a linen factory. The living is a p. curacy in the diocese of Norwich. Value, £88. Patron, L. Press, Esq. The church is ancient but good."*

http://www.visionofbritain.org.uk/place/7778

"In 1870-72, John Marius Wilson's Imperial Gazetteer of England and Wales described Fressingfield like this:

FRESSINGFIELD, a parish in Hoxne district, Suffolk; 4 miles S by E of Harleston r. station, and 8½ W by N of Halesworth. It has a post office under Harleston. Acres, 4, 560. Real property, £9, 273. Pop., 1, 325. Houses, 290. The property is much subdivided. The living is a vicarage, united with the rectory of Withersdale, in the diocese of Norwich. Value, £597. Patron, Emanuel College, Cambridge. The church is ancient but good; has a tower and a porch; and contains a brass of 1489, and an altar-tomb of Archbishop Sancroft. There are a Baptist chapel, a national school, and charities £46. Archbishop Sancroft was a native, and also died here."*

http://www.visionofbritain.org.uk/place/7210

Geall Green
125.posted 26 Sep 2018, 21:20

Nephew had a new hint which bizarrely wasn't shared with me (or my kids). He obviously is more of a Green than we are.

Predicted relationship: Distant Cousins
Possible range: 5th - 8th cousins

Confidence: Moderate

DNA Match
7th cousin 1x removed of Nephew

As the match is via Stephen Green the connection via me is:-

DNA Match
7th cousin
Father of DNA Match
Laurence Geall (1911 -)
Grandfather of DNA Match
Edith Eliza Barbara Kemp (1877 -)
Mother of Laurence Geall
Ann Bradford (1854 -)
Mother of Edith Eliza Barbara Kemp
Ann Olive (1830 -)
Mother of Ann Bradford
Eliza Green (1811 -)
Mother of Ann Olive
William Green (1774 -)
Father of Eliza Green
Stephen Green (1740 - 1809)
Father of William Green

Really a very distant match. Had Edith Kemp in my tree, her descendants are new. Edith marrying a Geall and one that came from Ripe, intrigued me. Was there a Geall connection too? I got as far back as Charles Geall, 1794 but no trace of his parents. A potential gave his father as William Geall, 1762. Potential Hints now give source information. The source for William Geall is "*Hills & Vales (Draft) DNA, created by Sue Skinner*".

William Geall was already in my tree, found another connection!

William Geal (1762 -)
6th great-uncle
Thomas Geall (1735 -)
Father of William Geal
Ann Geall (1765 - 1845)

Daughter of Thomas Geall

William is now also:-

William Geal (1762 -)
great-grandfather of husband of 4th cousin 3x removed
Charles Geal (1794 - 1844)
Son of William Geal
George Geal (1837 -)
Son of Charles Geal
John Geall (1877 -)
Son of George Geal
Edith Eliza Barbara Kemp (1877 -)
wife of John Geall
Ann Bradford (1854 -)
Mother of Edith Eliza Barbara Kemp
Ann Olive (1830 -)
Mother of Ann Bradford
Eliza Green (1811 -)
Mother of Ann Olive
William Green (1774 -)
Father of Eliza Green
Stephen Green (1740 - 1809)
Father of William Green

Laurence Geall (grandfather of DNA match) via Green is my 5th cousin 2x removed or via Geall is my 4th cousin 3x removed

The DNA Match that was a 7th cousin via Green is now:-

DNA Match
6th cousin 1x removed
Father of DNA Match
Laurence Geall (1911 -)
Grandfather of DNA Match
John Geall (1877 -)
Father of Laurence Geall

George Geal (1837 -)
Father of John Geall
Charles Geal (1794 - 1844)
Father of George Geal
William Geal (1762 -)
Father of Charles Geal
Thomas Geall (1735 -)
Father of William Geal
Ann Geall (1765 - 1845)
Daughter of Thomas Geall
Thomas Barber (1793 - 1862)
Son of Ann Geall
Eleanor Barber (1825 - 1867)
Daughter of Thomas Barber

Kemp
126.posted 26 Sep 2018, 22:42

I went to attach the wedding doc for Ann Bradford to James Kemp and she
was already there. For some reason I had never looked at his hints before
today. What I want to sort out is how they are connected to each other. (how
I miss that calculator!) In 1871, they are both living with William Winter in
Seaford. Ann is his niece and James is his grandson. ?

Originally:-

James W Kemp (1851 -)
3rd cousin 4x removed
Ann Winter (1827 -)
Mother of James W Kemp
Barbara Green (1805 - 1869) William Winter (1805-1891) husband of Barbara
Mother of Ann Winter
William Green (1774 -)
Father of Barbara Green
Stephen Green (1740 - 1809)
Father of William Green

Now also:-

James W Kemp (1851 -)
husband of 3rd cousin 4x removed
Ann Elizabeth Bradford (1854 - 1936)
wife of James W Kemp
Ann Olive (1830 -)
Mother of Ann Elizabeth Bradford
Eliza Green (1811 - 1873)
Mother of Ann Olive
William Green (1774 -)
Father of Eliza Green
Stephen Green (1740 - 1809)
Father of William Green

Great Niece
127. posted 26 Sep 2018, 23:18

Ann Elizabeth Bradford is the great niece of William Winter not his niece meaning she is second cousin of her husband James William Kemp. Had to draw that to sort it in my head.

Robbins
128.posted 6 Oct 2018, 09:43

When I first had my test I had this Robbins link:-
https://sites.google.com/site/theashleaze/genealogy/research-blog/finalmatch

My nephew has a match and the shared matches are to the person above (my 4th cousin 1x removed) and my first cousin but not to me or my children. ?!? This match is a cousin of my 4th cousin 1x removed, sharing Herbert Robbins as their grandfather. I only had to add the match, rest obviously already in my tree.

Predicted relationship to Nephew: 4th Cousins

Possible range: 4th - 6th cousins
Confidence: Very High

DNA Match Robbins
4th cousin 1x removed to me
DNA Match Father (1922 - 2005)
Father of DNA Match Robbins
Herbert Harold Robbins (1901 - 1971)
grandfather of DNA Match
Arthur Nelson Robbins (1876 - 1965)
Father of Herbert Harold Robbins
Job Robbins (1852 - 1896)
Father of Arthur Nelson Robbins
William Robbins (1821 - 1883)
Father of Job Robbins
William Robbins (1788 - 1845)
Father of William Robbins

Speaking of my first cousin, her father died recently and despite not knowing my Uncle, I went to his funeral. Was a bit weird going to a funeral of someone you don't know. Also weird meeting Aunts, Uncles and cousins you haven't seen for 35 years or so.

Brenchley Luckhurst
129.posted 7 Oct 2018, 17:41

Nephew had a distant match with someone when I searched for matches to Luckhurst. The only Luckhurst in the matches tree was a Sarah Ann Luckhurst but he had no details for her apart from marrying a Jacob Brenchley. His whole Brenchley line came from Kent, specifically Faversham, Charing, Stalisfield and Doddington.

My husbands adopted line of Brenchleys come from Kent too, specifically Milsted, Faversham and Charing.

This person had to be connected to these Brenchleys?

First of all, had to see if Sarah Luckhurst was the DNA connection to nephew. Sarah Ann Luckhurst was born c1836 in Little Chart, Kent. She was baptised on the 18th January 1837, her parents are Edward and Sarah Luckhurst. Sarah married Jacob Brenchley in Lenham in 1855 and they went on to have at least 6 children.

I got back on this line quite far:-

> **Robert Luckhurst (1670 -)** Kent (guess)
> John Luckhurst (1695 -) Married in Biddenden, Kent
> Son of Robert Luckhurst
> Richard Luckhurst (1730 -) Married in Biddenden, Kent
> Son of John Luckhurst
> Richard Luckhurst (1756 -) Married in Bethersden, Kent
> Son of Richard Luckhurst
> Edward Luckhurst (1794 -) Lived in Little Chart, married in Westwell
> Son of Richard Luckhurst
> Sarah Ann Luckhurst (1836 -)
> Daughter of Edward Luckhurst

But no connection found to Nephews Luckhurst line. His came from Bredhurst, Harbledown and Faversham.

Couldn't get very far back on the Brenchleys so no connection found their either.

> **Daniel Brenchley (1789 -)** Stalisfield, Charing, Little Chart
> Jacob Brenchley (1835 -) Little Chart, Lenham
> Son of Daniel Brenchley
> Edward J Brenchley (1873 -) Lenham, Doddington
> Son of Jacob Brenchley
> Stanley Edward Brenchley (1899 - 1974) Faversham
> Son of Edward J Brenchley

Look at the locations though! So very similar. Very frustrating. I went from two possible matches and an amusing family connection to nothing.

I look at many matches which come to nothing and I don't normally type them up. This one though I was so sure I would find something, I though it worth saving the fail for posterity.

Worth noting the DNA match goes back another 5 generations on his Brenchley line.

Holmden
130.posted 8 Oct 2018, 21:49

Very pleased with this, only had Frances without a surname earlier:-

Reynold Homden (1575 -)
12th great-grandfather of nephew
George Holmeden (1600 -)
Son of Reynold Homden
George Holmeden (1639 -)
Son of George Holmeden
George Holmeden (1660 -)
Son of George Holmeden
George Holmeden (1687 -)
Son of George Holmeden
Frances Holmeden (1733 -)
Daughter of George Holmeden
John Loveland (1759 - 1808)
Son of Frances Holmeden
Frances Loveland (1790 -)
Daughter of John Loveland
Mary Ann Steer (1810 - 1876)
Daughter of Frances Loveland
Eliza Smith (1831 - 1901)
Daughter of Mary Ann Steer
John Tucknott (1864 - 1949)
Son of Eliza Smith

The surname fluctuated between Holmeden and Holmden and ended up with Homden. There was some interesting spellings of Reynold. Reynold

Homden was Renold and Renald. His grandson George called his first son George and the second son was Reynold and this tradition carried on for the next 3 generations.

They come from Limpsfield and Crowhurst.

"In 1870-72, John Marius Wilson's Imperial Gazetteer of England and Wales described Limpsfield like this:

LIMPSFIELD, a village and a parish in Godstone district, Surrey. The village stands 6 miles NE of Godstone r. station, and 12 ENE of Reigate; and has a postoffice under Red Hill. The parish contains also Moorhouse, Tenchley, and Trevereux. Acres, 3,904. Real property, £5,384. Pop., 1,216.

Houses, 245. The property is divided among a few. The manor belongs to G. W. G. Leveson Gower, Esq. Hookwood, adjoining the village, is the seat of Mrs. Gower; Tenchley Park is the seat of Seymour Teulon, Esq.; Moor House is the residence of J. F. Harris, Esq.; and Trevereux is the property of H. Cox, Esq. A house near the centre of the village was long occupied by Mrs. Stanhope, the writer of well known published letters to her husband, Philip Stanhope, the natural son of Lord Chesterfield. A picturesque common, clumped with firs, lies above the village; and other parts of the parochial surface are diversified and beautiful. Staffords-Wood is a favourite resort of gypsies. The living is a rectory in the diocese of Winchester. Value, £699. Patron, W. Leveson Gower, Esq. The church is mainly early English, in good condition; has a tower, possibly Norman, with a piscina in the S wall, and surmounted by a spire; comprises nave, N aisle, and chancel; and contains a fine marble monument to Lord Elphinstone. There are a Baptist chapel, national and infant schools, and charities £4."*

http://www.visionofbritain.org.uk/place/4336

"In 1870-72, John Marius Wilson's Imperial Gazetteer of England and Wales described Crowhurst like this:

CROWHURST, a parish in Godstone district, Surrey; on Broad-Mead water and the Southeastern railway, 2½ miles ESE of Godstone r. station, and 9½ E by S of Reigate. Post town, Godstone, under Red Hill. Acres, 2,081. Real property, £1,707. Pop., 211. Houses, 40. The manor belonged, from an early period till the 18th century, to the Gaynesfords; and the manor-house, called Crowhurst Place, now a farm-house, was a stately mansion of the time of Henry VII.

Another farm-house was the seat of the Angell family, a mansion of the time of Henry VIII. The living is a vicarage in the diocese of Winchester. Value, £65. Patron, the Earl of Cottenham. The church has parts from transition Norman to perpendicular English; and contains brasses of the Gaynesfords. A hollow yew tree in the churchyard measures 30¾ feet in girth at five feet from the ground; and is the largest in the county."

http://www.visionofbritain.org.uk/place/4085

Peoples Vote
131.posted 20 Oct 2018, 23:19

Well in about 5 months we are due to leave the EU. This month we are supposed to be finalising the deal. But it is impossible because of the Brexit Travel Paradox:-

(I have no idea where to source that from, some logo top left - facebook snip)

The latest idea is that the exit is delayed by a couple of months until this is sorted. Of course the Brexiteers don't want this. Unlikely to happen cos if

112

someone could sort out the Northern Ireland situation in 2 months wouldn't they have done so years ago??

Today, around 670,000 people took part in a march to ask for a 'Peoples Vote' on whatever deal Theresa May finally gets. As much as I am a remainer, I don't get it. It's not a second referendum to decide again. It's just agreeing whatever crap deal she gets. The remainers will vote no cos they don't want to leave. The brexiteers will vote no cos it will be too European so the result would be no. Then we reject the deal and leave with no deal. How can that be better?

Though I don't see how no deal would resolve the Brexit Travel Paradox.

Winifred Moore
132.posted 22 Oct 2018, 18:40

I have recently been contacted by someone who is descendant from Samuel Silvester Moore. I am not sure if I should point her to any posts here cos they aren't likely to help her. The contact has given me an extra daughter though; Winifred. Apparently she was born after he died. Samuel died in Dorset in 1881, so Winifred was born either 1881 or 1882. The only birth hint is in Lewisham in the last half of 1882. A search in Dorset doesn't bring up anything. Like some of her siblings I cannot find her arrival details either. So what I have is:-

Winifred emigrated from England c1900 as she was living in Ingham, Herbert, Queensland in 1903. She was working as a music teacher. Winifred may have travelled back to the UK on the *Orama* as someone with her name arrived in London on the 13th September 1913. If Winifred did go to the UK she was back in Australia working as a stenotypist? By 1925, Winifred was working as a journalist and she was living in Merthyr, Brisbane.

Winifred died on the 11th November 1952 in Queensland. The death doc describes her as a 'spinster journalist'.

It would appear from a google search that she worked for The Brisbane Courier. She was also a founding member of the National Parks Association of Queensland.

http://www.womenaustralia.info/exhib/cal/moore.html
http://www.womenaustralia.info/biogs/AWE2894b.htm

1914-1918
133.posted 13 Nov 2018, 19:56

To commemorate the end of WW1 I did these for each line. I only got to save Maddox on here. I went to do Paterson and lost the WW1 tree in the process. I can't reupload it as it isn't on this computer. Doh! I was then too nervous to upload the other ones as those trees were much more involved.

Donald Trump did not attend the ceremony in France because it was raining. I cannot say anything else on that, that has not been said already.

Well they said November. And it appears the UK and EU have agreed text of the draft withdrawal agreement. I want to know how they solved the Brexit Paradox! Interesting to note "the Irish government said negotiations were "ongoing and have not concluded"."

On Wednesday Theresa takes it to the cabinet, at the same time the EU countries will discuss. If it gets through those two hurdles then it is up against the Parliament vote. Of course the major Brexiteers are saying its rubbish and they will vote no. This is just the withdrawal agreement for next couple of years. Still no clue what happens after that.

It seems positive (as positive as I can be as a remainer):-

"Northern Ireland's Democratic Unionist Party, which gives Theresa May vital support in key votes, said it would be a "very, very hard sell".

But Conservative Chief Whip Julian Smith said he was "confident" it would get through Parliament.

The future of the border between Northern Ireland and the Republic of Ireland has been the last major outstanding issue to be settled amid disagreements over how to guarantee that there will not be physical checks reintroduced after Brexit.

The draft agreement also includes commitments over citizens' rights after Brexit, a proposed 21-month transition period after the UK's departure on 29 March 2019 and details of the so-called £39bn "divorce bill"."

https://www.bbc.co.uk/news/uk-politics-46188790

Politics
134.posted 15 Nov 2018, 20:04

I don't get it. I don't understand why the withdrawal deal is of importance. It should have been - in 4 years we will leave, we'll pay you a bit of the divorce money each time a new trade agreement made, in 4 yrs we'll pay the balance of the divorce money. During those 4 years, everything will stay the same. Not two years discussing what the next two years is going to be like with no clue about new trade agreements for after that. There appears to be only one law known "At the end of the transitional period, UK environmental law will have to be at least on a par with the EU" which is a good thing but I'd rather have my food safety/standard laws at least on a par with the EU.

The document is 585 pages long so I have used the Beebs handy guide:-
https://www.bbc.co.uk/news/uk-politics-46208764

Basically its taken them 2 years to decide that everything stays the same for next 2 years apart from bizarrely (or not when you think about your classic gammon face) "*On farming, the UK won't be tied to the Common Agricultural Policy after March 2019.*"

My Brexit fears are just delayed from March 2019 to December 2020.

Of course that's if May gets it through. Because as it is, to all intents and purposes remaining for another 18 months, all of the Brexiteers are up in arms and resigning.
Shelley
135.posted 1 Dec 2018, 17:15

New DNA line match for me. Nice as confirms the stained glass windows at St Nicholas Church and the Grade II cottage :) Already had to Jeanie Edwards.

Predicted relationship: 4th Cousins
Possible range: 4th - 6th cousins
Confidence: Good

DNA Match
3rd cousin 2x removed
Leslie Samuel Walbourn
Father of DNA Match
Jeanie Edwards (1885 -)
Mother of Leslie Samuel Walbourn
Jane Shelley (1846 -)
Mother of Jeanie Edwards
John Shelley (1818 - 1875)
Father of Jane Shelley
Mary Shelley (1846 - 1924)
Daughter of John Shelley
William Alfred Snelling (1873 - 1912)
Son of Mary Shelley

Hannah Mitchell
136.posted 2 Dec 2018, 09:26

William Shelley married Elizabeth Julia Myers on the 21st October 1829. They had a daughter, Clara, in 1832. Clara Shelley was baptised at St Nicholas' on the 30th September 1832.

There is no trace of Clara in 1841. Her father and mother are living with a couple of her older half siblings. Clara is working as a servant in Stepney in 1851. There is no trace of her again in 1861. On the 7th September 1869, a Clara Shelley marries a Thomas How. The father of this Clara is a bootmaker

116

not a sexton. Wondering if 'my' Clara actually died before 1841 and this is a different Clara. However this other Clara was born in Brighton too.

In 1871, this Clara and her husband are living in Lambeth. Also with them is a Hannah Catherine Mitchell born in Ballarat East, Victoria, Australia in 1864. Whether this is my Clara or not, this explains the absence in the 1861 census. Clara must have gone to Australia between 1851 and 1861 and returned with a daughter before 1869. There are no immigration documents in either England or Australia to confirm this. The Australian birth docs give her father as a William Mitchell. There is no evidence of a marriage between a William Mitchell and a Clara Shelley in either country. When Clara marries Thomas she says she is a spinster.

Lots of questions.

In an aside I messaged the new DNA match - don't often do that. Wanted to know if they had seen the windows at St Nicholas'. They have.

The Americans
137.posted 8 Dec 2018, 14:08

Just done 6 seasons of The Americans this week. I probably watch too much telly! Binge watching box sets is how I spend my life.

I particularly liked this spy programme as it was a 'period drama' . Period being the '80s. I find it strange that I am so old now that my childhood is now a 'period drama'.

In the '80s, spies were proper spies. They did dead drops, used one time code pads, slept with people to get info, killed people and basically it seems exciting. Using phone booths too. Not being able to get hold of someone at any time is I guess, history now. We used to survive without mobiles!

Any drama about spying since the mid '90s is just watching someone hack into a satellite and position the satellite onto whoever they are watching. Or tracing their phones. Really not the same at all.

In other news, the Shelley DNA match has sent me a very long message that I need to look at. Sounds like my Shelley line is incorrect. I don't think I was ever particularly happy with it. I noted on the 15th December 2013 that there were 3 options and I sort of went for the Rustington one.

Rustington Shelley
138.posted 8 Dec 2018, 16:53

Delete Delete!!

So I did think that William Shelley was born on 5th July 1871 in Brighton. Made more sense than Rustington but with no documentation to suggest otherwise I went for it. This is what I had. I have just disconnected the parents William Shelley and Ann Pollard rather than deleting all of them.

John Shelley
11th great-grandfather
John Shelley (1633 - 1681)
Son of John Shelley
John Shelley (1655 -)
Son of John Shelley
John Shelley (1683 -)
Son of John Shelley
John Shelley (1716 -)
Son of John Shelley
William Shelley (1759 -)
Son of John Shelley
William Shelley (1782 - 1872)
Son of William Shelley

Cosstick
139.posted 19 Dec 2018, 13:23

The daughter of this DNA match contacted me recently. She is also in contact with the great great grandson of the cricketer Sam Cosstick but I am not coming up as a DNA match to him.

The Cosstick DNA is obviously very diluted as it is basically going back to 6th or 7th Green ancestor so not surprised that we aren't coming up as a match. But why do I come up as a match to the other person? I think it relates to Jane Sage Hubbard but I cannot find her birth docs on family search so have no evidence either way.

Shelley Update
140.posted 19 Dec 2018, 13:50

The cousin has sent me lots of documents to back up her theory.

1. Elizabeth Newnham baptism entry (confirming 1st Nov 1757 Clapham)
2. An illegible 1790 baptism entry (probably George Shelley)
3. George Shelley (1790) banns entry (confirming marriage entry 14 Aug 1812 to Edith Brazier St Nicholas' Brighton)
4. Will of George Shelley (this is the evidence for her theory but haven't looked at it yet - pages of tiny old writing hard to read)
5. Obituary of William Shelley (awesome!)
6. John Shelley baptism entry (confirming a John Shelley in Southwick 1751 - BUT - how do we know it isn't 1743 West Firle or 1746 Rustington?)
7. John Shelley banns entry (confirming marriage entry 16th May 1774 to Elizabeth Newnham)

In addition she also mentioned that William Shelley and Mary Thorn also had another child called William born out of wedlock and baptised on the same day that they got married - 17th April 1808. I cannot find a bastard William Thorn/Shelley but there is a William Thorn - parents William & Mary Thorn baptised on that date. I think it is unlikely that these are the same people. I don't think that St Nicholas church would get William (Snr)'s surname wrong. In addition there is no trace of William Thorn/Shelley (Jnr) after this baptism doc. Of course William (jnr) might have died before 1841 census. Though I think my contact has this name in a will indicating he was still alive in 1826 at least.

Peripatetic Purveyor of News
141.posted 19 Dec 2018, 14:10

Peripatetic means 'travelling from place to place'.

I liked the obituary of William Shelley. Firstly because it was in print so I could read it without trouble but mostly because it gave me pre census information about work he did prior to being a sexton and also gave some background into his life towards the end. He seems to have had a famous friend. Somers Clarke (if he is George Somers Clarke) was an architect and Egyptologist that did work on some Brighton churches, though not St Nicholas'. His wiki page.

I do not know what newspaper this is or the date of his funeral to work out when this was published - sometime around mid July 1872 anyway.

<u>William Shelley Newspaper Obituary Transcription</u>

DEATH OF MR. WILLIAM SHELLEY.

Mr William Shelley, the venerable sexton of this parish, and who had held his office for upwards of 54 years, died at his residence, Mount Sion-place, on Saturday morning last. Mr Shelley was a native of Brighton, and at the time of his death was in his 91st year, having been born in the year 1781. In the year 1807-8 Mr Shelley was on the staff of this journal; he was, in fact, the first Brighton newsman, his beat being to the westward, through Shoreham, Steyning, etc., as far, we believe, as Storrington. In those days of slow travelling, none, he has told us, were more cordially welcomed, in the towns and villages through which he passed, that the original peripatetic purveyor of news. Mr Shelley subsequently filled the office of Town Crier; which he relinquished in 1818, on receiving the appointment of Parish Sexton from Dr. Carr, the then Vicar of Brighton, and subsequently Bishop of Chichester. Throughout his long life Mr Shelley enjoyed excellent health; but about 12 years ago he became nearly blind from cataract. An operation, however, having been successfully performed, and his sight restored, he was almost a "young man" again; at all events, the pleasure of once more beholding familiar faces seemed to give him new life and spirits. On the 5th of October, last year, his 90th birthday, Mr Shelley accepted an invitation from his sons to a supper at the "Morning Star," and at which he responded to the toast of his health with extraordinary vivacity and cheerfulness, considering his advanced age. In honour of the day, several touches of grandsire triples were rung by the Brighton Society of Change Ringers from the old tower of St. Nicholas. Up till within the last few weeks, Mr Shelley might be seen almost daily in the Pavilion Grounds — his favourite place of resort — as pleased as ever to have a chat with old friends; he, however, experienced some difficulty in walking. Mr Shelley's sufferings during his last illness were at times very acute; but his death was tranquil, taking place, as above stated, in the presence of several members of his numerous family, by whom he had been affectionately tended during illness. His medical attendant was Mr Crawford J Pocock; and all that skill and unremitting attention could do was done to alleviate his sufferings, though from the first it was felt that the case was hopeless. In his last illness Mr Shelley was frequently visited by the Vicar, and by the Revs. J.J. Hannah and C.S. Chilver; the Rev. T. Cooke, the Rev. T. Trocke, Mr Somers Clarke, and other friends have also evinced their respects by repeated visits. The funeral will take place this afternoon at three o'clock, when the mortal remains of the deceased will be interred in a family grave in the eastern part of the old church-yard. The funeral service will be performed by the Rev. Dr. Hannah (the Vicar) and the Rev. Thomas Trocke.

Deponent
142.posted 19 Dec 2018, 20:32

Deponent - a person who makes a deposition or affidavit under oath

Sort of guessed the meaning but thought I'd check.

George Shelley
143.posted 20 Dec 2018, 13:11

George Shelley is the son of John Shelley and Elizabeth Newnham, one of at least 8 children. He was baptised presumably at St Nicholas' on the 15th February 1790.

On the 14th August 1812, George married Edith Brazier. George and Edith had at least 5 children, 3 girls and 2 boys. After their last daughter Elizabeth Eliza was born in 1825, George presumably got ill. He wrote a will on the 26th September 1826, dying between that date and his burial on the 19th October 1826.

His will describes him as a 'victualler' so I presume he ran a pub. He definitely had land as the will refers to rental income from his properties plus the house he lived in.

The will says he is making his brother William Shelley (sexton - my Gt grandparent) and his friend George Sawyer executors (and their heirs should they die). He left these two people £10 each. This is the evidence that William Shelley's parents would be John Shelley and Elizabeth Newnham.

The rent proceeds of his properties would go to his wife Edith unless she died or remarried. The interest would be put into trust and split between his children when the youngest reaches 21. He also left £20 each to his sons to go towards any apprenticeship. His son George appears to have become a butcher and his son Henry became a groom.

On the 27th March 1827, Edith and William went for a meeting with George Proctor regarding the will. They both swore under oath that the will is as it was when written. I don't think this is a usual procedure so maybe there was some discussion over his will?

Transcripts
144.posted 21 Dec 2018, 07:27

I think what is weirdest about these documents is the lack of punctuation. No full stops ever. Random capital letters. Sentences that start with 'And' - though that suggests the previous sentence ever finished. Anyway:-

<u>George Shelley Will Transcript</u>

I George Shelley of Brighthelmston Victualler do declare this to be my last will and testament

I give unto my brother William Shelley and my friend George Sawyer the younger their Executors and Administrators all that my House and Premises in Russel(?) Place Brighton in the occupation of John Norris upon trust to pay the rents thereof unto my dear Wife

Edith for her life and after her Death to pay the Rents thereof and to sell and dispose of the same and pay the net monies thence arising as hereinafter mentioned.

*Also I give and devise unto the said William Shelley and George Sawyer their Heirs Executors and Administrators all the *est? and re*? my Estate and Effects whatsoever as well real as Personal upon the trusts following *? For the first place to pay all my just Debts and Funeral and Testamentary Expenses and the Legacies hereinafter bequeathed and subject thereto in h*? to pay the Rents Intact and Annual Proceeds thereof unto my said wife for her life or during so long as she shall continue my Widow and after her decease or marriage again. In trust to pay and divide all the said Rents Interest and annual proceeds unto and equally among all my children and the s*?? of such as may die; such issue taking only their parents share until the youngest of my children shall attain the age of Twenty one Years and when the youngest of my children shall attain that age the trust to sell and absolutely dispose of the residual of my and also the House before mentioned (after my wifes Death) said Estate and Effects in such manner as my Trustees may think most advantageous and ??? the net moneys thence arriving to pay and divide and equally among all my children who may be living at the time of my decease and the *?* of such of them as may be then dead (such *?* making only their parents share) and I died that in case of the death of either of my trustees the survivor and upon the death of the survivor his Heirs Executors and Admins shall and may have and exercise the same power and authorities ad are given to my said trustees jointly and that every Receipt of my Trustees a Trustee shall be an effectual discharge for the many therein mentioned to be received*

I appoint the said William Shelley and George Sawyer Executors of this my will to whom I bequeath the Sum of Ten Pounds apiece and consolidate them and my said wife Guardians of my children during their minority

I authorize my Trustees to pay Twenty Pounds apiece towards putting each of my Sons apprentice to any Trade or Business

In witness whereof I have hereunto by my hand seal this 26th day of September 1826

Signatures

Then the weird probate type affidavit document (the writing of George Proctor being particularly hard to read):-

Archdeaconry of Lewes in the County of Sussex } *On the twenty third day of March in the year of our Lord one thousand eight hundred and twenty seven*

??? personally Edith Shelley Brighton in the said County the Widow George Shelley late of Brighton aforesaid deceased and also William Shelley aforesaid Sexton, the son of William Shelley living one of the Executors named in the Last Will and Testament of George Shelley leaving date the twenty sixth day of September one thousand eight hundred and twenty six and first the said Edith Shelley was on oath that her late Husband the said George Shelley did shortly before his death de? to her the said Edith Shelley a ??? ??? ??? and widowed "The Will of /W. Geo Shelley" which he declared did contain his last will and testament and did desire her this deponent to help the ??? safely until after the funeral of him the said deceased and then to deliver the same of the said William Shelley and that this deponent did accordingly keep the said ??? until after the funeral of her late testament and did these deliver the same of the said William Shelley unopened(?) and exactly in the same state in which it had been delivered to this deponent by her said late Husband and the said William Shelley maketh oath that ??? from the said Edith Shelley a parcel(?) sealed and ??? as aforesaid which did contain the Will and Testament of the said George Shelley hereunto annexed(?) and he further maketh oath that at the time he first saw and read the said will the words "to pay the rents thereof and" were underlined between the eighth and ninth lines thereof and the words "and also the House before mentioned after my Wifes death" were underlined between the thirty first and thirty second lines thereof and that the said Will is now in every respect in the same (s)light and condition as it was at the time when this deponent first saw and read it*

Signatures Edith Shelley William Shelley

Sworn before me

George Proctor Surrogate

*23rd March 1827 There were(?) sworn William Shelley and George Sawyer the Executors in this Will *** to whom was committed the *** of the Execution thereof sworn also that the Goods Chattel and Credits of the deceased do not amount in Value unto Six hundred pounds*

By us

George Proctor Surrogate

124

Jermaine
145.posted 21 Dec 2018, 10:16

9 distant cousins had Jermain/Jermaine as one of their middle names so I thought I would go back on non blood line to see where it came from. The first instance of this as a middle name seems to be in 1799 but cannot see any reason for why it started or the continued use.

Thomas Lulham & Mary Cousens c1740 m c1760 had some children, none of which had Jermaine, one of their sons:-

Thomas Lulham & Ann (Arthur?) 1764 m c1798 had some children, the first born appears to be first use:-

Sarah Jermaine Lulham 1799

Thomas Lulham & Mary Ann Parkin 1818 m c1830 also son of Thomas & Ann also used it:-

Emily Mary Jermaine Lulham 1834

Frederick Lulham & Mary 1832 m c1865 son of Thomas & Mary used it too:-

Edith Jermaine Lulham 1869

Sidney Lulham & Jane 1837 m c1858 another son of Thomas & Mary used an exact previously used name:-

Emily Mary Jermaine Lulham 1859

Horace Lulham & Elizabeth Burrell 1842 m c1870 another son of Thomas & Mary are what started this off:-

Lillian Maud Jermaine Lulham 1871–1955
Horace Vernon Clair Jermaine Lulham 1872–1950

Elizabeth Winnifred Jermain Lulham 1875–1955
Sidney Burrell Jermain Lulham 1876–1957
Mabel Louise Jermain Lulham 1878–1967
Cecil Howard Jermain Lulham 1879–1906
Leslie Bertram Jermain Lulham 1883–1919
Dorothy Ivy Jermain Lulham 1885–1957
Doris Jermain Lulham 1890–1970

Mad. Nearly a hundred years and 3 generations.

Robbins
146.posted 11 Jan 2019, 20:13

Think the Xmas DNA gifts are starting to come in. I have two close cousins come up but without shared match. First one was easy as I already had his mother in my tree.

Predicted relationship: 4th Cousins
Possible range: 4th - 6th cousins
Confidence: Extremely High

DNA Match
4th cousin
Mother of DNA Match (1910 - 1969)
Ada Mary Robbins (1884 - 1952)
Grandmother of DNA Match
James Robbins (1844 - 1919)
Father of Ada Mary Robbins
William Robbins (1821 - 1883)
Father of James Robbins
William Robbins (1788 - 1845)
Father of William Robbins
Isaac Robbins (1828 - 1889)
Son of William Robbins
Joseph Henry Robbins (1869 - 1919)
Son of Isaac Robbins

The next one is frustrating as they only have 11 people in their tree. Shared matches show it is Paterson side. Only common surname is Llewellyn.

Predicted relationship: 3rd Cousins
Possible range: 3rd - 4th cousins
Confidence: Extremely High

The match is obviously Welsh and that part of my tree is very hard to do. Wondering whether to message them or not to see if they have anything else.

I also got some DNA kits for Xmas. I got an Ancestry one to test my Mum and I got a 23andme one for me. I did get my Mum to spit in the tube on Xmas Day but I haven't done anything with it yet. Despite waiting half hour after drinking it did seem to look like Baileys... I haven't actually done anything as I have been either ill or busy since then.

Shute
147.posted 12 Jan 2019, 11:01

I spat in the 23andme test, added the stabilizer and then spilt it. I think that is 2 tests ruined now but they have both been posted so just have to wait and see. I wonder how many tests are sent that can't be processed?

That Llewellyn possibility has raised another query re Isaac & Jane and appendix 10/appendix 10 v2. I think a Mary Ann Llewellyn married a George Allen in Swansea in 1902. (note spelling is Lewellin) If my Ann Llewellyn is the Great Aunt of Mary Ann Llewellyn then the DNA match will be my 4th cousin 1x removed rather than a 3rd cousin. The match might come up as being closer because I would be linked to Jane as well as Ann.

Sighs
148.posted 15 Jan 2019, 07:49

Remember that MP vote on the deal? Got postponed and then there was Xmas. There has been so many arguments and squabbles and it is just so frustrating. You wonder if the politicians do it on purpose so that the public

just don't care anymore. My social media (where political) is definitely remain
so I am used to seeing all the crap that they post. However I have 2 old (70+)
friends who are posting leave stuff and it is very strange to see that. I want
to go aghhhhh you have ruined my country but they are nice people (even if
I now know misguided!).

Bets on what will happen in the vote that is finally happening today? I can't
see it getting through.

33
149.posted 15 Jan 2019, 11:57

Son and nephew are now both at 33 shared matches and I am now at 32. Our
new match has a private tree so cannot say what the connection is but pretty
sure it is just another Barber match. Have messaged the person to see if they
will share their tree.

The Llewellyn contact confirmed his grandmothers dob and location but it
didn't help. Name is too common.

230
150.posted 16 Jan 2019, 01:25

Brexit plan has been rejected by 230 votes - the largest defeat for a sitting
government in history.

MPs voted by 432 votes to 202 to reject the deal, which sets out the terms of
Britain's exit from the EU on 29 March.

19
151.posted 17 Jan 2019, 08:20

So Jeremy called for a vote of no confidence. As *'Have I Got News For You'*
joked:- "MPs likely to reject Corbyn's vote of no confidence in PM, as the
only thing they have less confidence in than her is him."

128

MPs have voted for Theresa May's government to continue, rejecting Labour's motion of no confidence by 325 votes to 306. MPs have voted entirely along party lines, resulting in a majority of 19 in support of Theresa May's government. Good. First thing they have done in last two years that makes sense. If we have to vote again I want it to be a referendum not a general election. A general election would not resolve anything as (apart from my party that nobody votes for) no party is either remain or leave.

In more interesting news, the DNA match shared her tree and the connection (again) was Barber. I had to Blaine already:-

Predicted relationship: Distant Cousins
Possible range: 5th - 8th cousins
Confidence: Good

DNA Match
5th cousin
Barber
Mother of DNA Match
Blaine Wallace Barber (1930 -)
Grandfather of DNA Match
Benjamin Wallace Barber (1889 - 1975)
Father of Blaine Wallace Barber
James Arthur Barber (1867 - 1958)
Father of Benjamin Wallace Barber
Benjamin Barber (1828 - 1899)
Father of James Arthur Barber
Thomas Barber (1793 - 1862)
Father of Benjamin Barber

Charlotte Pell x2
152.posted 25 Jan 2019, 21:53

I was randomly searching for DNA matches and put in Thornton. It came up with one which I clicked on but it also had Pell as a shared name. It wasn't Thornton but it seemed likely it was Pell. However I only had a Charlotte

Pell born 1823 and died 1824. The match had her born in 1834 and marrying a Henry Ross Shelbourn. (without parents) It didn't help that the 1841 census was mistranscribed and had the whole family as Leeson rather than Pell.

I didn't have to do a convoluted search to find a link as I had actually written a note on 1823 Charlotte "1881 census, mother is Visitor at Shelborn's - Charlotte Shelbourn - daughter?"

Why I didn't think that she had two daughters at the time I wrote that note I really don't know. I seem to have done quite a poor job on the children of George Pell and Ann Barber (not those Barbers). The bold are the additional children added this evening:-

Elizabeth Pell 1821–
Charlotte Pell 1823–1824
Sarah Pell 1825–
Thomas Pell 1828–
Ann Pell 1830–
Joseph Pell 1832–1896
Charlotte Pell 1834–1908
John Pell 1837–1838
John Pell 1839–
Alice Pell 1841–
Frances Pell 1843–1924

Pell link doesn't seem strong:-

Predicted relationship: Distant Cousins
Possible range: 5th - 8th cousins
Confidence: Good

However:-

DNA Match
4th cousin
Alice Mary Shelborn (1912 - 1989)
Grandmother of DNA match

130

Charles Shelborn (1871 -)
Father of Alice Mary Shelborn
Charlotte Pell (1834 - 1908)
Mother of Charles Shelborn
George Pell (1799 - 1866)
Father of Charlotte Pell
Frances Pell (1843 - 1924)
Daughter of George Pell

9th
153.posted 26 Jan 2019, 17:41

This has got to be the MOST distant match surely? (*only it's not* - it is a tie*)

Predicted relationship: Distant Cousins
Possible range: 5th - 8th cousins
Confidence: Moderate

DNA Match
9th cousin
Franklin Tuppen (1907 -)
Grandfather of DNA Match
Richard Tuppen (1875 -)
Father of Franklin Tuppen
Richard Tuppen (1847 -)
Father of Richard Tuppen
John Tuppen (1815 -)
Father of Richard Tuppen
William Tuppen (1787 -)
Father of John Tuppen
William Tuppen (1763 -)
Father of William Tuppen
William Tuppen (1731 -)
Father of William Tuppen
Susan Clapson (1705 -)
Mother of William Tuppen
Benjamin Clapson (1671 - 1750)

Father of Susan Clapson
Mary Clapson (1708 -)
Daughter of Benjamin Clapson
John Hoad (1735 - 1824)
Son of Mary Clapson
Thomas Hoad (1772 - 1838)
Son of John Hoad
Sarah Hoad (1796 - 1838)

Susan Clapson and all of the Tuppen descendants are new to my tree. On familysearch, Benjamin & Mary Clapson had 3 sons between 1695-1720; Thomas 1697, Joseph 1699 and Benjamin 1701. It doesn't have my Mary (1708) or their Susan (1705). The 'evidence' I have that Benjamin and Mary are Marys parents is a Millennium File and their 'evidence' is a public tree. However I have another* 9th cousin from Benjamin Clapson so I can only assume familysearch is incomplete or the girls were never christened or the documents were lost or destroyed.

Benjamin Clapson
154.posted 26 Jan 2019, 19:56

Benjamin and Mary actually had 6 children, another son, John was born in 1714.
This is from *http://theweald.org/N10.asp?NId=30080016* :-

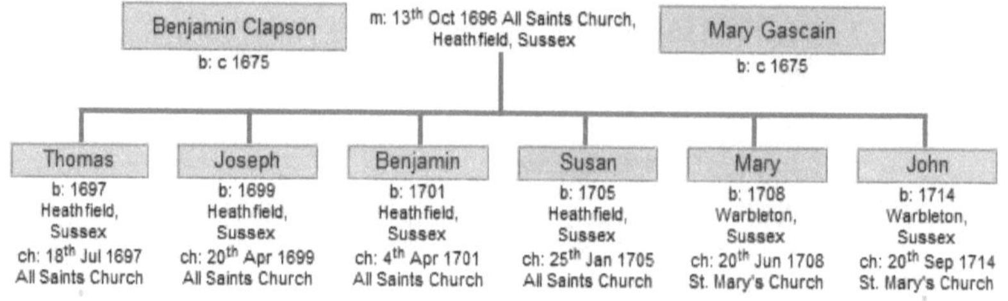

Goodey
155.posted 1 Feb 2019, 07:53

Son has a match to the Hoad line but no shared match with us 3 which is strange being a Green line. From the recent Hoad work, I had to Mabel Hollands already but had got no further because as I now know she emigrated to New Zealand.

    Predicted relationship: Distant Cousins
    Possible range: 5th - 8th cousins
    Confidence: Moderate

    DNA Match
    4th cousin 2x removed of ME (4th cousin 3x removed of son)
    Mabel Florence Hollands (1882 -)
    Grandmother DNA Match
    William Hollands (1843 -)
    Father of Mabel Florence Hollands
    Ruth Hoad (1804 - 1855)
    Mother of William Hollands
    Thomas Hoad (1772 - 1838)
    Father of Ruth Hoad
    Sarah Hoad (1796 - 1838)
    Daughter of Thomas Hoad

The most fantastic programme has been on recently, so funny. Danny Dyers Right Royal Family. Over 2 programmes it showed him looking at his ancestors from King Rollo to some Seymour woman. It is a follow up to the WDYTYA episode when he discovered he was descendant from Edward III. (II?) It wasn't about learning history, that side was more basic than Horrible Histories, it was how he dressed up and reacted to what he was doing. I always thought Danny Dyer was a bit of a twat with his OTT Cockneyisms but I really warmed to him, he was great. So much better than Lucy Worsley dressing up. That always seems weird.

So 1st Feb - less than 2 months to go before Brexit and nothing but politicians arguing continues. Theresa went to EU to ask for changes. They said no.

We are going to Paris soon, in my mind travelling for the last time as a European. Though I can pretend for another 10 years as I just got my passport renewed.

William Scotney
156.posted 2 Feb 2019, 08:54

Searched for Scotney and 3 matches came up, 2 of which were Bourne so thought likely connection. They both had a William Scotney as an ancestor which tied in to my William Scotney though I only had my ancestor Elizabeth in the tree. Firstly went on familysearch to see what other children William had and think (with a question on 2 Williams) there are 9 children:-

Charles Scotney 1782–
Elizabeth Scotney 1784–1850
John Scotney 1786–
William Scotney 1787–
William Scotney 1788–
Ann Scotney 1790–
Mary Scotney 1792–
Sarah Scotney 1793–
Frances Scotney 1796–

The first match was quite easy (semi following their tree combined with hints):-

Predicted relationship: Distant Cousins
Possible range: 5th - 8th cousins
Confidence: Moderate

DNA Match
5th cousin 1x removed
Ethel Mary Darby (1888 -)
Grandmother of DNA Match
Emily King (1863 -)
Mother of Ethel Mary Darby
Joseph King (1830 -)
Father of Emily King
Frances Scotney (1796 -)
Mother of Joseph King

William Scotney (1758 -)
Father of Frances Scotney
Elizabeth Scotney (1784 - 1850)
Daughter of William Scotney
William Turfitt (1814 - 1859)
Son of Elizabeth Scotney

The second match was harder because the son of John (1786) Scotney according to the match and most of the documentation was John (1828) but familysearch had a baptism in 1840. Either this baptism was a different John or John Snr either waited 12 years to baptise John Jnr or he called 2 sons John.

Predicted relationship: Distant Cousins
Possible range: 5th - 8th cousins
Confidence: Moderate

DNA Match
5th cousin 1x removed
Nellie Scotney (1897 -)
Grandmother of DNA Match
Arthur Scotney (1866 -)
Father of Nellie Scotney
John Henry Scotney (1828 -)
Father of Arthur Scotney
John Scotney (1786 -)
Father of John Henry Scotney
William Scotney (1758 -)
Father of John Scotney

Two More
157.posted 2 Feb 2019, 20:30

First one was easy enough as already had to William Green:-

Predicted relationship: Distant Cousins
Possible range: 5th - 8th cousins
Confidence: Moderate

DNA Match
7th cousin
Annie Green (1908 -)
Grandmother of DNA Match
William Green (1878 -)
Father of Annie Green
Alfred Green (1854 - 1899)
Father of William Green
Stephen Green (1817 - 1908)
Father of Alfred Green
Stephen Green (1795 - 1863)
Father of Stephen Green
Henry (Harry) Green (1772 - 1846)
Father of Stephen Green
Stephen Green (1740 - 1809)
Father of Henry (Harry) Green

Next one was strange as it was predicted to be shared 6th+ grandparent and turned out to be shared 3rd gt grandparents. I already had to Albert and he had unlooked at hints. I want to look into Albert as one of his daughters was born in India. The match also confirmed the wife of Frederick Taylor is Mary Stapleton as her granddaughter has Stapleton as a middle name:-

Predicted relationship: Distant Cousins
Possible range: 5th - 8th cousins
Confidence: Moderate

DNA Match
2nd cousin 2x removed
Jessie Stapleton Taylor (1914 - 1991)
Grandmother of DNA Match
Albert Alexander Taylor (1874 - 1947)
Father of Jessie Stapleton Taylor
Frederick Taylor (1837 -) (wife Mary Stapleton)
Father of Albert Alexander Taylor
Mary Annie Taylor (1872 - 1967)
Daughter of Frederick Taylor

The Taylor/Stapleton gene must be pretty weak in me.

Albert Alexander Taylor
158.posted 3 Feb 2019, 11:44

A Taylor. Such an impossible name to find records for. I also really seem to struggle finding out what units of the Army do and where they went.

Albert was the son of Frederick Stapleton and Mary Stapleton. He was born on the 15th October 1874 and baptised at St Nicholas on the 28th September 1875. He lived in Brighton until at least 1894 where he worked as a plumber.

On the 28th February 1894 he signed up to the 1st Sussex Artillery Volunteers. This was a part time unit of the Royal Artillery. They worked on coastal defences so it seems very unlikely that they would have been based abroad. Albert was 5ft 9 3/4" weighed 152 lbs, had brown eyes and brown hair with a fair complexion. He also had a scar on his left temple.

All of his postings do not have a location, the first of which was on the 10th January 1895. On the 25th June 1904 Albert married Lizzie Frances Ganday and they had a son the following year after he was promoted to Corporal on the 11th April 1905. Then before 1907, Albert and Frances went to India as their two daughters were baptised in Sialkot, Bengal. (Dorothy born 22/2/1907, baptised 24/3/1907 and Iris born 15/8/1908, baptised 6/9/1908)

On the 14th May 1908, presumably whilst in India, Albert got promoted to Sargeant. It is not clear when the family returned from India but Albert left the army on the 30th June 1912. He received a pension of 13.5p per diem and was living at 119 South Harbour Street. (This area - if Brighton - is now posh flats by the marina)

According to his WW1 pension record, he was recommended for a GC medal on the 8th January 1913. I am assuming this was for long service good conduct rather than a George Cross. Can't find evidence of either. In 1914, Albert and Frances have another daughter; Jessie. When WW1 started he would have been 39/40. Due to his past military history I assume he served rather than considered too old. He signed up to the Royal Artillery unit 2910 but I do not know what they did in the war.

In 1939 he was living in Brighton and working as a stationers porter. Albert was living at 73 Whichels Place, Brighton, when he died on the 8th August 1947. He left £547 19s 7d to his wife.

(73 Whichelo Place still exists in Brighton - maybe probate had slight typo?)

https://en.wikipedia.org/wiki/1st_Sussex_Artillery_Volunteers

Ann Hartley
159.posted 3 Feb 2019, 21:29

Ann was the daughter of John Hartley and she was baptised on the 17th April 1756 at Morton nr Bourne. On the 29th March 1781 she married William Phillips. Ann & William presumably had many children between 1781 and 1797 but the surname Phillips is too common to check. On the 22nd March 1797, their daughter Hartley Phillips was baptised. Hartley married John Scotney on the 28th January 1828.

John and Hartley had at least 5 children, one of which was James Hartley Scotney c1837. James married Sarah Ann Studd and of their 8 or more children, one was John Hartley Scotney c1874. James and Sarah also had a son called Charles. He married Alice Mary Steward and one of their children was called Cyril Hartley Scotney 1909. James and Sarah also had a daughter called Fanny. She married Henry Robert Carter and one of their children is called George Frank Hartley Carter 1910.

Slow
160.posted 9 Feb 2019, 12:59

Must have been a lot of DNA xmas presents, finally got notification that results are expected by 2nd March! I have got so used to a speedy service that waiting this long seems strange. I hope this means that it isn't Baileys and the

138

sample is ok. The 23andme is even slower, only just got email to say that one has been received.

In other news, I am meeting my cousin today so that he can show me the grave of Joseph. I had attempted to find it several years ago but as it isn't marked I couldn't find it.

Beckenham 2
161.posted 10 Feb 2019, 00:16

Can't believe it was 5 years ago on the 10th May 2014 that I went looking for the grave of Joseph. I had arranged to meet my cousin at 2. It had been a nice but very windy day. It started spitting and then by the time we got to the grave it was a torrential downpour.

The grave is slightly sunken/overgrown and currently, as you would expect, covered in leaves. It has a border with an inscription on that was still legible; "In loving memory of Joseph Charles Paterson July 2nd 1920 aged 66 years". My cousin had been there a couple of days before with a trowel to clear the ground so that the inscription could be seen. We then had a wander to the Commonwealth Graves part of the cemetery. As we started walking back the rain stopped so we then looked at the graves of the famous people buried at Beckenham Crem; Carey Blyton, William Walker, Thomas Crapper, Frederick Wolseley, Samuel Rowbotham & W G Grace.

Think I will probably go to the grave again on the 2nd July 2020, to mark the centenary of his death. My cousin showed me some useful landmarks to locate it that I took photos of, so fingers crossed I can find it by myself.

Me
162.posted 17 Feb 2019, 16:18

Thing I hate most about having my problems is that he takes everything as being my problem when I could be well and have a valid issue. Which is actually 90% of the time. I think this exasperates the other 10% of the time.

Not Baileys
163.posted 21 Feb 2019, 21:00

Mums results are in. I don't know if it is too early but she has zero shared ancestor hints which is weird. Everyone else had them come up straight away. She should have loads that are the same as mine. However she does have 299 4th cousins or closer! (In comparison, I have 171, nephew has 168, son has 197, daughter has 154 and husband has 165.) Maybe that is why the shared hints are taking a long time? From my quick scan of the 4th cousins or closer, there is one new Barber (there's a surprise) but also a 2nd cousin I don't know about. He has no info so I need to message him. From the shared matches I would say Green is the connection.

On the ethnicity side, England, Wales & Northwestern Europe 89%, Ireland and Scotland 6% and Germanic Europe 5%.

I have also found it interesting which of her grandchildren take after her the most, it is my son with 2,055 cm across 69 segments. Then it is my daughter with 1,489 cm across 50 segments (quite a drop) and following closely behind her, my nephew is 1,432 cm across 40 segments. Big difference son and nephew. My Mum is more closely related to her cousin; 1,710 cm over 60 segments than 2 of her grandchildren. All four of them are referred to as Possible range: Close family - 1st cousins, Confidence: Extremely High.

I obviously come up as Possible range: Parent, Child - immediate family member, Confidence: Extremely High with 3,463 cM across 66 segments.

Straight Hair
164.posted 21 Feb 2019, 22:58

23andme results also in. First report I went to was how Neanderthal I am. Seems quite a bit but only on 1 of the 4 indicators:-

Highest in 23andMe - 397 Variants

Me - 301 Variants

140

"300+ variants Some of your traits may be influenced by having Neanderthal variants.

Scientists at 23andMe identified associations between Neanderthal variants and certain physical traits. If you have certain Neanderthal variants, it means that some of your physical traits may trace back to your Neanderthal ancestors."

Variant(s) found:-

A Straight hair You have 1 Neanderthal variant associated with having straighter hair.

B Less likely to sneeze after eating dark chocolate You have 0 Neanderthal variants associated with a reduced tendency to sneeze after eating dark chocolate.

C Less back hair You have 0 Neanderthal variants associated with having less back hair.

D Height You have 0 Neanderthal variants associated with your height."

Now to look at the health report....

George Green
165.posted 22 Feb 2019, 09:05

Taken a while to find a new match but this is quite a good one, being the first that confirms George Green as my 3rd Gt Grandfather . There are no shared matches which is why not come up for me or the grandchildren. I had John Green already, his son George Allen and his descendants are from the match:-

Predicted relationship to Mum: 4th Cousins
Possible range: 4th - 6th cousins
Confidence: High

DNA Match
4th cousin to me (3rd cousin 1x removed to Mum)
George Allen Green (1928 - 1984)
Grandfather of DNA Match
John Green (1889 -)

Father of George Allen Green
George Green (1851 - 1918)
Father of John Green
George Green (1817 - 1886)
Father of George Green

Mary Suter
166.posted 22 Feb 2019, 10:59

Another Timothy Suter confirmation. I had Mary Suter in my tree with some hints I hadn't looked at. I am very interested in Ward Meadows but Ancestry is playing up. He seems to have had 15 children, moved inbetween Canada, Ireland, India and several locations in England.

Predicted relationship: Distant Cousins
Possible range: 5th - 8th cousins to Mum
Confidence: Moderate

DNA Match
4th cousin 1x removed of me (3rd cousin 2x removed of Mum - so closer than predicted)
Alfred Wallace Meadows (1895 - 1950)
Grandfather of DNA Match
Ward Meadows (1835 - 1919)
Father of Alfred Wallace Meadows
Mary Suter (1808 - 1841)
Mother of Ward Meadows
Timothy Suter (1772 - 1851)
Father of Mary Suter

Ward Meadows
167.posted 22 Feb 2019, 13:06

Ward was born in Brooke, Rutland and baptised there on the 28th October 1838. He was the son of John Meadows, an ag lab, and Mary Suter. Haven't found the source of the name 'Ward' yet. In 1851, aged 13, he was working as a 'day boy'. At some point he then joined the Army. It appears that there

142

might be some records on Fold3 regarding his service but I don't have that. I think he was with the 58th (Rutlandshire) Regiment of Foot. Info on wikipedia regarding the Victorian era of this regiment does not exactly tie in with the birth locations of his children so it might not have been.

https://en.wikipedia.org/wiki/58th_(Rutlandshire)_Regiment_of_Foot

In 1864 he was in Montreal, Canada. Ward married Elizabeth Balchin at Presbyterian Saint Gabriel at this time. They had 2 or 3 children in Ontario between 1866 and 1869 before returning to England. (Only one survived and not sure whether 3rd was born in Canada or Farnham). In 1871, he was based in Colchester Barracks working as a Drill Sargeant and they had another son. Ward and Elizabeth had another 4 children in various locations between 1872 and 1878 before going to Nantwich in Cheshire. I think at this point he had received an injury of some sort as he went into the Chelsea Pensioner hospital on the 25th March 1879 for an examination. In 1881, Ward was working as "Head Army Pensioner Instructor Cheshire Rifle Volunteer". Ward stayed in Cheshire until at least 1887. Can't find anything specific about the Cheshire Rifle Volunteers as not sure which battalion he was instructing.

His wife Elizabeth was from Canada and they went to live in Manitoba Canada c1889. Not all of their living children went with them. In Canada he worked as a farmer and they had 4 more children. Ward and Elizabeth had at least 18 children!! (I have no documentation for their first son Edwin, his info comes from the DNA match but the birth date fits.)

Ward and Elizabeth returned to England presumably for a visit c1909 as they arrived back in Quebec on the 10th September 1909 on the Victoria.

Ward appears to have then lived in Brandon, Manitoba for the rest of his life, dying there on the 5th March 1919.

Birth locations of his 18 children:-

    (Edwin Ward 1866-1867 Ontario)
    David George 1867 London, Ontario
    Ward Albert 1869 (died 1870 Farnham, Surrey)
    Charles John 1871 Colchester, Essex
    Ward Henry 1872 Winchester, Hampshire

Elizabeth Mary 1874 Davenport, Devon
Alice Emma 1876 Cork, Ireland
Earnest William 1878 Agra, Utter Pradesh, India
Harry Frederick 1879 Nantwich, Cheshire
Maud May 1881 Nantwich, Cheshire
Lydia Beatrice 1882 Nantwich, Cheshire
Harriet Anne 1884 Nantwich, Cheshire
Arthur Claude 1886 Nantwich, Cheshire
Edith Mabel 1887 Nantwich, Cheshire
Reginald Edward 1891 Odanah, Manitoba, Canada
Walter Francis 1892 Minnesosa, Manitoba, Canada
Cecil Herbert 1893 Odanah, Manitoba, Canada (Roped City)
Alfred Wallace 1895 Odanah, Manitoba, Canada (Roped City)

Non Barber Geall
168.posted 22 Feb 2019, 15:20

Predicted relationship: Distant Cousins
Possible range: 5th - 8th cousins to Mum (*again not a match to anyone else*)
Confidence: Moderate

DNA Match Beech
6th cousin 1x removed to me (5th cousin 2x removed to Mum)
Walter Morris Beech (1904 -)
Grandfather of Beech
Lois Geal (1869 -)
Mother of Walter Morris Beech
William Geal (1836 -)
Father of Lois Geal
Henry Geal (1796 -)
Father of William Geal
Robert Geal (1769 -)
Father of Henry Geal
Thomas Geall (1735 -)
Father of Robert Geal

144

This match may also have a connection to Henty as well. In addition, the matches lines for Geall and especially Cruttenden are much longer than mine but unsure if they are just based on Millennium Files/Public Trees at present.

Cruttenden Options
169.posted 22 Feb 2019, 18:12

The Cruttendens of Burwash continue to confuse. I have always gone with Joseph Cruttenden and Mary as the parents of Mary Cruttenden 1731. See Appendix 46 and previous Burwash post. This was despite the Millennium File having her parents as Thomas Cruttenden and Mary Hales/Haley.

The DNA Match has gone with Thomas and Mary and I wanted to see if her tree was correct because she had this line going back to a John Culpeper in 1140!!

My first go gives the father of Thomas as Thomas and does not go back to the key person of Joan Byne:-

William Cruttenden (1600 -)
10th great-grandfather
Thomas Cruttenden (1634 -)
Son of William Cruttenden
Thomas Cruttenden (1661 -)
Son of Thomas Cruttenden
Thomas Cruttenden (1694 - 1763)
Son of Thomas Cruttenden
Mary Cruttenden (1731 -)
Daughter of Thomas Cruttenden

If I go with what the DNA match has which is equally possible I get:-

Goddard Cruttenden (1588 -)
10th great-grandfather
Goddard Cruttenden (1620 -)
Son of Goddard Cruttenden
Robert Cruttenden (1668 -)
Son of Goddard Cruttenden

Thomas Cruttenden (1694 - 1763)
Son of Robert Cruttenden
Mary Cruttenden (1731 -)
Daughter of Thomas Cruttenden

There is nothing for Goddard 1588. It is all just public trees. If his parents are Goddard and Judith Coney then the tree will look like this (plus a LOT more):-

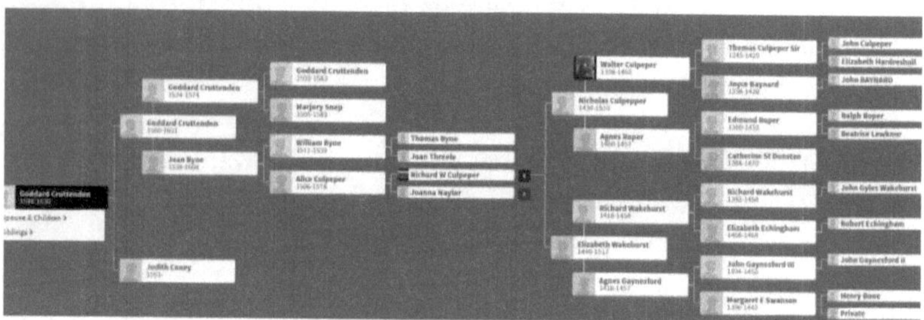

Hayler
170.posted 22 Feb 2019, 20:04

I had Robert Geal, the rest is all from the match:-

Predicted relationship: Distant Cousins
Possible range: 5th - 8th cousins to Mum (no shared)
Confidence: Moderate

DNA Match
7th cousin (6th cousin 1x removed of Mum)
Edith Maud Hayler (1913 -)
Grandmother of DNA Match
Edward Hayler (1882 -)
Father of Edith Maud Hayler
William Henry Hayler (1857 - 1920)
Father of Edward Hayler
Richard Hayler
Father of William Henry Hayler
Beulah Ruth Geal (1815 -)
146

Mother of Richard Hayler
Robert Geal (1769 -)
Father of Beulah Ruth Geal
Thomas Geall (1735 -)
Father of Robert Geal

Sherris
171.posted 23 Feb 2019, 08:10

Not sure if I had stopped writing up brothers marrying sisters as it happens so much but thought before doing loads more Cruttenden/Geal connections that I would. There are lots and surprisingly they are not Utah Barbers either.

Anyway, Reginald Edward Meadows married Emily Florence Sherris on the 9th December 1914. His brother, Walter Francis Meadows married Clara Gertrude Sherris on the 27th October 1920.

Mum now has 300 4th cousins or closer but still no shared hints.

Wilson
172.posted 23 Feb 2019, 15:46

I was very good this morning. After the last post, I turned computer off and did some washing and other housework. However after lunch I started again!

First up was another Richard Carley match, I had Stephen Carley but the rest is from matches tree:-

Predicted relationship: Distant Cousins
Possible range: 5th - 8th cousins of Mum (no shared)
Confidence: Moderate

DNA Match
5th cousin 1x removed of me (4th cousin 2x removed of Mum)
Edgar John Fullager (1868 -)

Grandfather of DNA Match
Mary Ann Carly (1839 -)
Mother of Edgar John Fullager
Henry Carley (1816 -)
Father of Mary Ann Carly
Stephen Carley (1782 - 1857)
Father of Henry Carley
Richard Carley (1735 - 1798)
Father of Stephen Carley
James Carley (1770 -)
Son of Richard Carley

Then I looked at a couple that apparently had no shared match but upon investigation I already had. Lots of that yesterday. I need some sort of system for knowing who I have done already and the ones I have looked at but can't find a link. I then searched a lot of surnames and was surprised to find a Sarah Wilson 1796 in Hatfield Broad Oak. I have not gone further than John Wilson and I didn't have Sarah Wilson. However, this match was a shared match with one of Mums Snelling cousins and therefore it seems sensible to assume that John and Sarah are siblings. Obviously Sarah & her descendants are all new from the matches tree:-

Predicted relationship: Distant Cousins
Possible range: 5th - 8th cousins of Mum (*shared with her Snelling cousin*)
Confidence: Moderate

DNA Match Streeton
5th cousin 1x removed of me (4th cousin 2x removed of Mum)
Martha E Elvey (1889 -)
Grandmother of DNA Match
Alfred Joseph Elvey (1863 -)
Father of Martha E Elvey
Joseph Elvey (1831 -)
Father of Alfred Joseph Elvey
Sarah Wilson (1796 -)
Mother of Joseph Elvey
Wilson
Father of Sarah Wilson
John Wilson (1801 - 1886)
148

Son of Wilson
Sarah Eliza Wilson (1839 - 1925)
Daughter of John Wilson
Sarah Wilson (1858 - 1930)
Daughter of Sarah Eliza Wilson

I hoped that I could match some christening docs to a town and location but Hatfield Broad Oak doesn't come up. The obvious choice was a Francis Wilson but his Sarah and John were born in Romford which is 23 miles away. Another option was a William Wilson in Leyton but that is further away and the dates aren't quite right. Of course they might not be siblings at all, they might share grandparents.

If Francis is right I can get back to William Wilson (1670 -) 8th great-grandfather to me.

John Wilson
173.posted 23 Feb 2019, 16:56

Whether the last match was correct or not, this one is a verification of the Wilson line. That makes me very happy as it was one of the few remaining Green lines that did not have a match. I did have Susan, sister of Sarah already but the rest is from the match. Also, the relationship is closer than predicted:-

Predicted relationship: Distant Cousins
Possible range: 5th - 8th cousins to Mum no shared
Confidence: Moderate

DNA Match Gunn
4th cousin 1x removed to me (*3rd cousin 2x removed to Mum*)
Henry Jason Gunn (1884 -)
Grandfather of DNA Match
Mary Ann Trundle (1858 -)
Mother of Henry Jason Gunn
Susan Wilson (1836 -) - *they have Susannah but same parents*
Mother of Mary Ann Trundle
John Wilson (1801 - 1886)

Father of Susan Wilson
Sarah Eliza Wilson (1839 - 1925)
Daughter of John Robert Wilson

Crimean War
174.posted 23 Feb 2019, 20:36

"In 1870-72, John Marius Wilson's Imperial Gazetteer of England and Wales described Hatfield Broad Oak like this:

HATFIELD-BROAD-OAK, or Hatfield-Regis, a village, a parish, and a sub-district in Dunmow district, Essex. The village stands on an eminence, at Pinceybrook, 4½ miles ENE of Sawbridgeworth r. station, and 5½ SE of Bishop-Stortford; is an ancient place; was formerly a market town; and has now a post office‡ of the name of Hatfield-Broad-Oak, under Harlow, and a fair on 5 Aug.

The parish is divided into the fonr quarters of Town, Brunsend, Heath, and Woodrow. Acres, 8, 810. Real property, £10, 941. Pop., 1, 960. Houses, 405. The property is subdivided. The manor belonged anciently to the Crown; was given, after the Conquest, to the De Gernons; passed to the Bruces, the Bohuns, the Staffords, the Riches, and the Barringtons; and belongs now to the faniily of Lowndes. The seat occnpied by the Bruces, and that occupied by the Barringtons, are now farm houses; and the former is moated, and belongs to the Earl of Roden. Barrington Hall was begnn about 1740, but not completed till 1864; and is now the seat of G. A. Lowndes, Esq. Down Hall, the seat of Sir John Sylwin, and Gladwyns, are good mansions. A Benedictine priory was founded in the parish, in 1135, by Aubrey de Vere; and given, at the dissolution, to T. Noke. The living is a vicarage in the diocese of Rochester. Value, £180. Patron, Trinity College, Cambridge. The church is later English, and good; has a lofty tower; and contains a fine effigies of Robert de Vere, third Earl of Oxford. The vicarages of Hatfield-Forest and Hatfield-Heath are separate benefices. There are an Independent chapel, a national school, and charitics £177. The snb district contains seven parishes. Acres, 21, 381. Pop., 4, 554. Houses,"*

http://www.visionofbritain.org.uk/place/6750

I have come to the conclusion that Epping seems to be the nearest birth district to Harlow/Great Dunmow/Hatfield Broad Oak. It doesn't really help with the parents of John Wilson and how John is connected to Sarah.

So back to looking at the real connection. Richard Trundle was born in Hatfield Broad Oak c1834. He lived with his parents in 1841. There is no trace of him in 1851, he has possibly joined the Army by this point. Richard was a Corporal in the 2nd Battalion Rifle Brigade. Regimental Number: 4046. He was awarded medals for service in Crimea, he was at the Battle of Alma on the 20th September 1854 and at the Battle of Inkerman on the 5th November 1854. When he left the Rifle Brigade he became an ag lab.

In 1856, Richard married Susannah/Susan Wilson. Richard and Susan had 6 daughters between 1858 and 1873. Finally they have a son, John, in 1876. There isn't a record of Susan after that. Maybe she died giving birth to John but I can't find a death doc. Richard lives with his children in White Roofing, Essex in 1881 and with his daughter and her family in 1891 in Matching, Essex. Richard died in 1898 in Dunmow.

Lorry
175. posted 24 Feb 2019, 11:07

Alice Trundle was born in 1867 in Hatfield Broad Oak.   Her youngest sister was called Emily and she married Frederick Robinson in 1894.

Alice lived with her family in 1871 and in 1881. In 1884, she married Jesse Cordell in Ongar, Essex. They went on to have 10 children between 1884 and 1907, 4 of which died in infancy. Most of her children were born in Ongar though later ones are registered to Epping. The 10 children were:-

Alice Ann - 1884 died
William - 1885 died
George - 15th March 1887
Alice Mary - 9th July 1892
Jesse - 1895
Arthur Louis - 1896 died
Minnie - 30th January 1898 (she married Christopher Jefferies and one of their children was a son called Graham)
Clifford John - 21st November 1900
Ellen - 26th November 1902
Leonard - 1905 died

At the end of 1929, not sure of exact dates, Alice was killed in an accident with a lorry. The following is a transcript of a newspaper clipping shared publicly on ancestry. I do not know the name of the newspaper or the date of the article. I do know I was very confused as to who her daughter Emily Robinson was until I realised that the article was incorrect and Emily was her sister not her daughter.

"LORRY'S STEERING FAILS

LOUGHTON WOMAN KILLED AT BISHOP'S STORTFORD

A sad motor accident occurred at Northgate End, Bishop's Stortford, on October 17, resulting in the death of Mrs. Alice Cordell, aged 63, of England's Lane, Loughton. She and her daughter, Mrs Emily Robinson, also of Loughton, were on a visit to another daughter, Mrs Minnie Jeffries, of Rye Street, Bishop's Stortford. They had been in the town marketing, and had with them Graham John Jeffries, the young son of Mrs. Jefferies. As they were returning along Northgate End at 5.20 pm, a motor lorry (belonging to Mr G E Rose of Bentfield Green Farm, Stansted, and driven by Mr. G B Camp of Bentfield Green), the steering gear of which suddenly went wrong, ran into them and crushed them against the wall. Police and doctors were quickly on the spot, and Mrs. Cordell was rushed in a motor ambulance to the Hospital, where she died on Friday morning. Mrs. Robinson and the boy were also taken to hospital, the former in a serious condition with a compound fracture of a leg and other injuries, and the boy, who had only been out of the hospital two days was suffering from a severe shock.

Mr Camp, the driver of the lorry, stated that as he was passing the Rising Sun his steering gear went wrong and the lorry swerved from the near to the offside across the path and onto the women.

At the inquest on Monday, evidence was given that the steering gear of the lorry was out of order, probably caused by a jolt owing to the bad state of the road at the spot. The jury returned a verdict of Accidental death, and exonerated the driver from blame. The Coroner said he concurred with the verdict, as he had driven over the road."

In an interesting WW2 aside, as I don't normally have WW2 info... Alice's grandson, Graham Jeffries, was a gunner in the 9 Coast Regiment of the Royal Artillery. His number was 1427395 and he served in Malaya. Graham was killed on the 16th March 1942. He is buried at Kranji War Cemetery in Singapore.

A Few More
176.posted 24 Feb 2019, 12:34

Think I have had enough. I need to go out, such a lovely sunny day. Have found a couple I already had this morning plus these 3, another Barber and 2 more Greens. I have some more Cruttendens to look at plus some Kimber investigating. The last Green one is a new match to John Green which is good plus first time Green is the surname the whole way through so included the whole connection for that one. (Prediction to Mum but relationship to me.) Most people in all 3 were already in my tree, just grandparents and below needed adding.

Predicted relationship: 3rd Cousins - *lots of shared Barber matches*
Possible range: 3rd - 4th cousins
Confidence: Extremely High

DNA Match
4th cousin 1x removed
Elmer Barber (1898 - 1989)
Grandfather of DNA Match
Julia B Barber (1860 - 1951)
Mother of Elmer Barber
Benjamin Barber (1828 - 1899)
Father of Julia B Barber
Thomas Barber (1793 - 1862)
Father of Benjamin Barber

Predicted relationship: Distant Cousins
Possible range: 5th - 8th cousins
Confidence: Moderate

DNA Match

7th cousin 1x removed
Annie Holmes Costick (1891 -)
Grandfather of DNA Match
Alfred Costick (1864 -) *married cousin Sophia Costick
Father of Annie Holmes Costick
William Costick (1832 - 1905)
Father of Alfred Costick
Samuel Costick (1792 - 1875)
Father of William Costick
Mary Green (1767 - 1848)
Mother of Samuel Costick
Henry Green (1736 -)
Father of Mary Green
John Green (1712 - 1770)
Father of Henry Green
Stephen Green (1740 - 1809)
Son of John Green

Predicted relationship: Distant Cousins
Possible range: 5th - 8th cousins
Confidence: Moderate

DNA Match
5th cousin 1x removed
Arthur Green (1890 -)
Grandfather of DNA Match
William Green (1852 -)
Father of Arthur Green
John Jarvis Green (1821 - 1899)
Father of William Green
John Green (1789 -)
Father of John Jarvis Green
John Green (1763 -)
Father of John Green
Jesse Green (1786 - 1873)
Son of John Green
George Green (1817 - 1886)
Son of Jesse Green
Albert Green (1853 - 1914)

Son of George Green
Mark Green (1875 - 1935)
Son of Albert Green
Ronald Green (1924 - 1958)
Son of Mark Green

Private
177.posted 24 Feb 2019, 19:44

I think I have sussed why Mum has no shared ancestor hints. As an adult, she had to have her own account to register her kit. I was assigned the manager and I linked the kit to my tree. Just assumed that would be it. I think nothing comes up as my tree is set to private. So I have sent invite to Mum to be a guest to my tree. Hopefully that should work.

Nope
178.posted 26 Feb 2019, 20:45

That didn't resolve, still zero hints. Have sent a message to Ancestry asking for help.

Thrulines
179.posted 1 Mar 2019, 07:28

AGHHHHH. I HATE the use of 'THRU'

Ancestry has a new feature called ThruLines and it is sort of like shared ancestor hints but laid out differently. It seems to have replaced DNA Circles which I never used. I am not sure if it is just directing to 'potential' ancestor hints which on the whole are nonsense. Or if true, cannot be validated.

It's the 1st March. Brexit is nearly upon us. Not that anyone knows what is happening. There have been a couple of pathetic political things which are too little too late. Finally Jeremy has said he would be ok with another referendum (with no time left to implement so he is safe there) and then a few mid centre remainers have left the Labour and Tory parties to form an independent group. Hello? Lib Dems??? As I said 2 years ago all remainers should go to Lib Dems and then there might have been a decent opposition to this farce.

Edward Stapleton
180.posted 1 Mar 2019, 10:00

ThruLines seems to be a useful tool, though as it is based on trees I am not sure how it differs to a shared ancestor hint. (Mum still has zero of those, I think it is because she doesn't pay for membership.) ThruLines is laid out nicely and it has enabled me to do nothing of any importance for the last couple of hours :)

First thing is it 'only' goes back to 5th Gt Grandparents so matches further away than 6th cousin won't come up. (For my daughter some 5th gt grandparents didn't come up like Barber but maybe she has no Barber in her?)

I have not looked at the Barber matches. They will be time consuming especially if I did them from my Mum:-

ThruLines suggests that I may be related to 28 DNA matches through Thomas Barber.
ThruLines suggests that Mum may be related to 130 DNA matches through Thomas Barber.
ThruLines suggests that Son may be related to 29 DNA matches through Thomas Barber.
ThruLines suggests that Nephew may be related to 50 DNA matches through Thomas Barber.

ThruLines has given me 2 new ancestor confirmations. The first of which I need to look into further as I can't tie it all together at the moment, re Job Taylor to investigate 6th cousin 7cm/1 segment. But I could tie in:-

New confirmation of Edward Stapleton
5th cousin 1x removed
14cm/1 segment

DNA Match

156

5th cousin 1x removed
Charles H Streeter (1894 -)
Grandfather of DNA Match
Mary Ann Thompson (1858 -)
Mother of Charles H Streeter
William James Thompson (1832 -)
Father of Mary Ann Thompson
Eleanor Stapleton (1812 - 1855)
Mother of William James Thompson
Edward Stapleton (1775 - 1856)
Father of Eleanor Stapleton
John Stapleton (1822 - 1899)

Various
181 posted 1 Mar 2019, 10:15

These are ancestors already confirmed by a previous match:-

3rd cousin 1x removed 11cm/1 segment

DNA Match
3rd cousin 1x removed
Donald Llewellyn (1927 -)
Grandfather of DNA Match
Thomas Llewellyn (1896 -)
Father of Donald Llewellyn
Emily King (1876 -)
Mother of Thomas Llewellyn
John King (1830 - 1888)
Father of Emily King
Harriet King (1865 -)
Daughter of John King

4th cousin 6cm/1 segment
nothing from John* private tree

DNA Match
4th cousin

Grandmother of DNA Match
John Hessett (1850 -)*
Father of a Hessett
Elizabeth Pell (1821 -)
Mother of John Hessett
George Pell (1799 - 1866)
Father of Elizabeth Pell
Frances Pell (1843 - 1924)
Daughter of George Pell

4th cousin
7cm/1 segment

A DNA Match Etsch
4th cousin
Alice Weldon (1897 -)
Grandmother of DNA Match
George Weldon (1864 -)
Father of Alice Weldon
Alice Pell (1841 -)
Mother of George Weldon
George Pell (1799 - 1866)
Father of Alice Pell
Frances Pell (1843 - 1924)
Daughter of George Pell

4th cousin 1x removed
12cm/1 segment

DNA Match Folkes
4th cousin 1x removed
Reginald Edward Meadows (1891 -)
Grandfather of DNA Match
Ward Meadows (1838 - 1919)
Father of Reginald Edward Meadows
Mary Suter (1808 - 1841)
Mother of Ward Meadows
Timothy Suter (1772 - 1851)
Father of Mary Suter

Eliza Suter (1819 - 1854)
Daughter of Timothy Suter

4th cousin 1x removed
7cm/1 segment

DNA Match
4th cousin 1x removed
Emma Meadows (1883 -)
Grandmother of DNA Match
David Meadows (1841 -)
Father of Emma Meadows
Mary Suter (1808 - 1841)
Mother of David Meadows
Timothy Suter (1772 - 1851)
Father of Mary Suter
Eliza Suter (1819 - 1854)
Daughter of Timothy Suter

5th cousin
12cm/1 segment

DNA Match
5th cousin
Beryl Stone
Grandmother of DNA Match
Walter Stone (1887 -)
Father of Beryl Stone
Frances Victoria Trundle (1865 - 1946)
Mother of Walter Stone
Susan Wilson (1836 - 1876)
Mother of Frances Victoria Trundle
John Wilson (1801 - 1886)
Father of Susan Wilson
Sarah Eliza Wilson (1839 - 1925)
Daughter of John Wilson

And a to do list:-

Charlotte Pell descendants Shelbourne to investigate 4th cousin 7cm/1 segment
plus on a different line 3rd cousin 1x removed 25cm/3 segments and 14cm/1 segment
A Robert Suter to look into another 4th cousin 1x removed 9cm/2 segments
ThruLines suggests that Sarah Paterson may be related to 18 DNA matches through Robert Pell.
Emma Harris to look at 5th cousin 6cm/2 segments (match tree set to private)
Elizabeth Carley to look at 5th cousin 1x removed 8cm/1 segment
Mary Freer private tree
Annie Meakin 2 5th cousins to look at

Jesse Green
182 posted 1 Mar 2019, 14:43

Another tick for a Green Ancestor:-

4th cousin (to Mum)
11cm/1 segment

DNA Match
4th cousin 1x removed to me
Dorothy E Green (1890 -)
Grandmother of DNA Match
Daniel Green (1850 -) *wife born Hong Kong (looks like Army family)*
Father of Dorothy E Green
Daniel Richardson Green (1822 - 1860)
Father of Daniel Green
Jesse Green (1786 - 1873)
Father of Daniel Richardson Green
George Green (1817 - 1886)
Son of Jesse Green

Meakin
183. posted 1 Mar 2019, 17:32

Harriet Swain is from Leicestershire. I have some investigating to do but it looks like 2 of her children went to Utah. This is a mad coincidence as it is the other Barber line. Eliza Meakin arrived in Boston on the Commonwealth on the 8th August 1902 and ended up in Utah, dying there on the 5th November 1929. Her younger brother Edward left the UK earlier, he arrived in the US in 1888. He married in Utah and died in Idaho.

Other Barber Line
4th cousin 2x removed (to Mum)
6cm/1 segment

DNA Match
5th cousin 1x removed
Norman Laverne Balmforth
Grandfather of DNA Match
Joseph Balmforth (1894 -)
Father of Norman Laverne Balmforth
Annie Meakin (1872 - 1906)
Mother of Joseph Balmforth
Harriet Swain (1827 -)
Mother of Annie Meakin
Mary Barber (1803 -)
Mother of Harriet Swain
John Barber (1778 - 1861)
Father of Mary Barber
Ann Barber (1800 - 1888)
Daughter of John Barber

Other Barber Line
4th cousin 1x removed (to Mum) x2
13cm/1 segment

Both DNA Matches
5th cousin
Grandfather of DNA Match
Annie Meakin (1872 - 1906)
Mother of Earnest Rudolph Balmforth

Harriet Swain (1827 -)
Mother of Annie Meakin
Mary Barber (1803 -)
Mother of Harriet Swain
John Barber (1778 - 1861)
Father of Mary Barber
Ann Barber (1800 - 1888)
Daughter of John Barber

Other Barber Line
4th cousin 1x removed (to Mum) x2
8cm/1 segment and 13cm/1 segment

Both DNA Matches
5th cousin
Grandmother of DNA Match
Annie Meakin (1872 - 1906)
Mother of Vera Balmforth
Harriet Swain (1827 -)
Mother of Annie Meakin
Mary Barber (1803 -)
Mother of Harriet Swain
John Barber (1778 - 1861)
Father of Mary Barber
Ann Barber (1800 - 1888)
Daughter of John Barber

In addition, have another Timothy Suter via Meadows:-

4th cousin 1x removed (to Mum)
8cm/1 segment

DNA Match
5th cousin
William Ward Meadows (1917 -)
Grandfather of DNA Match
Earnest William Meadows (1878 - 1947)
Father of William Ward Meadows

Ward Meadows (1838 - 1919)
Father of Earnest William Meadows
Mary Suter (1808 - 1841)
Mother of Ward Meadows
Timothy Suter (1772 - 1851)
Father of Mary Suter
Eliza Suter (1819 - 1854)
Daughter of Timothy Suter

Next up for checking is Banks.

Nicholls & Hubbard
184. posted 2 Mar 2019, 08:55

Two more new ones:-

5th cousin to Mum
10cm/1 segment

DNA Match
5th cousin 1x removed
Barnard
Grandfather of DNA Match
Charlotte Tucknott (1855 -)
Mother of Barnard
Thomas Tucknott (1818 -)
Father of Charlotte Tucknott
Sarah Hubbard (1788 -)
Mother of Thomas Tucknott
Nicholas Hubbard (1755 -)
Father of Sarah Hubbard
Jane Hubbard (1784 - 1848)
Daughter of Nicholas Hubbard

5th cousin to Mum
11cm/1 segment

DNA Match
5th cousin 1x removed
Katie Nicholls Barnard (1906 -)
Grandmother of DNA Match
Emma Nicholls (1866 -)
Mother of Katie Nicholls Barnard
William Nicholls (1825 -)
Father of Emma Nicholls
John Nicholls (1801 -)
Father of William Nicholls
John Nicholls (1768 - 1832)
Father of John Nicholls
Thomas Sayer Nicholls (1803 - 1853)
Son of John Nicholls

Ann Hode
185. posted 2 Mar 2019, 17:53

This next match has frustrated me for a while (been an obvious match when searching for Hoad) because as far as I was concerned, John and Susannah Hoad did not have a daughter called Ann. ThruLines lays the match out a bit better and so I could understand what it was implying. FamilySearch had nothing for Ann Hoad. However searching under the parents names, an Ann HODE came up. Having finally established the connection, I now have another ancestor.John Hoad, ticked off!

6th cousin to Mum
14cm/2 segments

DNA Match
6th cousin 1x removed
Gwendoline Cecila Wooller (1909 -)
Grandmother of DNA Match
Horace Wooller (1881 -)
Father of Gwendoline Cecila Wooller
Jabez Wooller (1853 -)
Father of Horace Wooller
Eliza Pont (1821 -)

Mother of Jabez Wooller
Ann Hode (1780 - 1855)
Mother of Eliza Pont
John Hoad (1735 - 1824)
Father of Ann Hode
Thomas Hoad (1772 - 1838)
Son of John Hoad

There will also be another confirmation coming from Martha Pont rather than Eliza Pont. The other one is 6th cousin to Mum, 17cm/1 segment.

Gasson & Carter
186.posted 2 Mar 2019, 20:07

Two more ancestors confirmed from Mums ThruLines and that is the last. Due to sheer volume of matches now, I will only write up another if it is a new confirmation. (As those lists of people are pretty dull to read) However, I will still add the matches to my tree. I do still have ThruLines for my paternal lines and then my nephew, son and husband to do. However they seem a bit messed up and don't seem to include all lines. Mums ThruLines was really useful and I'm going to do a snip of the Stephen Green matches.

5th cousin 1x removed to Mum
11cm/1 segment

DNA Match
5th cousin 2x removed
Alice Mary Watson (1888 -)
Grandmother of DNA Match
Mary A Furminger (1846 -)
Mother of Alice Mary Watson
Sarah Gasson (1822 -)
Mother of Mary A Furminger
John Gasson (1774 -)
Father of Sarah Gasson
James Gasson (1750 -)
Father of John Gasson
Sarah Gasson (1776 - 1844)

Daughter of James Gasson
Sarah Hoad (1796 - 1838)
Daughter of Sarah Gasson

5th cousin 1x removed to Mum *(wrong - match tree missing a generation I think?)*

6cm/1 segment

DNA Match
6th cousin 1x removed
John Noah Barnes (1875 - 1952)
Grandfather of DNA Match
Henry Barnes (1843 -)
Father of John Noah Barnes
Emma Carter (1823 -)
Mother of Henry Barnes
Sarah Carter (1799 -)
Mother of Emma Carter
James Carter (1776 -)
Father of Sarah Carter
John Carter (1743 -)
Father of James Carter
Hannah Carter (1773 - 1845)
Daughter of John Carter

Ann Pollard
187. posted 3 Mar 2019, 10:04

I decided to just quickly look at the women in case anything else came up and there was something for Ann Pollard. Due to an earlier match, I had disconnected Rustington William Shelley and Ann Pollard from my tree. This match was through Zacharias Shelley - that MUST mean the Rustington line is correct so I have reconnected them.

5th cousin 1x removed
13cm/1 segment

DNA Match
5th cousin 2x removed
Henry Thomas Farndell (1881 -)
Grandfather of DNA Match
Frances Carpenter (1856 -)
Mother of Henry Thomas Farndell
Frances Shelley (1818 -)
Mother of Frances Carpenter
Zacharias Shelley (1793 - 1845)
Father of Frances Shelley
William Shelley (1759 -)
Father of Zacharias Shelley
William Shelley (1781 - 1872)
Son of William Shelley
John Shelley (1818 - 1875)
Son of William Shelley
Mary Shelley (1846 - 1924)
Daughter of John Shelley

Common Ancestors
188. posted 5 Mar 2019, 09:08

Ancestry DNA Matches has had a revamp. It's quite good with some useful new features. It has a custom group category that I think might be helpful for husband paternal workings. It doesn't seem to matter that the shared ancestor hints don't appear for Mum, there appears to be something better; Common Ancestors. It is a filter. It would be helpful if the filters did exclude as well.

So whereas husband has 12 shared ancestor hints - he has 31 common ancestors
Daughter has 10 shared ancetor hints and 40 common ancestors
Son has 34 shared ancestor hints and 75 common ancestors
Nephew has 33 shared ancestor hints and 78 common ancestors
And finally Mum with 0 shared ancestor hints has 228 common ancestors

228! Too many. Think continuing to add DNA match cousins to tree is not going to happen. I will probably look at any non Mum related.

Traits
189. posted 8 Mar 2019, 15:55

Hadn't posted up any 23andme stuff since the Neanderthal bit so:-

Sleep and wake-up time

Deep Sleep	Less likely to be a deep sleeper	Yep
Sleep Movement	Likely average or less movement	Yep
Wake-Up Time	Likely to wake up around 7:51 am	I wish

Food and weight

Genetic Weight	Predisposed to weigh about average	Can only blame myself!
Lactose Intolerance	Likely tolerant	Yep
Saturated Fat and Weight	Likely similar weight	From diets I would concur
Bitter Taste	Likely can taste	Yep
Cilantro Taste Aversion	Slightly higher odds of disliking cilantro	(Coriander = soapy = not sure)
Sweet vs. Salty	Likely prefers salty	Yep

Wellness

Alcohol Flush Reaction	Unlikely to flush	Yep
Caffeine Consumption	Likely to consume more	Yep
Muscle Composition	Common in elite power athletes	Who knew?

Traits

Ability to Match Musical Pitch	About a 50/50 chance of being able to match a musical pitch	= NOPE
Asparagus Odor Detection	Likely can smell	Think so
Cheek Dimples	Likely no dimples	I do have one
Cleft Chin	Likely no cleft chin	Yep
Earlobe Type	Likely detached earlobes	Yep
Earwax Type	Likely wet earwax	Yep
Eye Color	Likely blue or green eyes	Mixture inc grey n brown specs/changeable
Fear of Heights	More likely than average to be afraid of heights	= a bit
Finger Length Ratio	Likely ring finger longer	Yep
Freckles	Likely a lot of freckles	Yep
Hair Photobleaching	More likely to experience hair photobleaching	- a bit
Hair Texture	Likely straight or wavy	Straight
Hair Thickness	Less likely to have thick hair	It used to be
Light or Dark Hair	Likely light	First proper WRONG - dark
Misophonia	More likely to hate chewing sounds	= ABSOLUTELY
Mosquito Bite Frequency	Likely bitten more often than others	- 50/50, not sure if more
Motion Sickness	More likely to experience motion sickness	- only if MIGRAINE
Newborn Hair	Likely little baby hair	Yep
Photic Sneeze Reflex	Likely no photic sneeze reflex	Yep
Red Hair	Likely no red hair	Hmmm, ginge when young
Skin Pigmentation	Likely lighter skin	Yep
Toe Length Ratio	Likely big toe longer	Yep
Unibrow	Likely no unibrow	I wish, 20 years of waxing...
Widow's Peak	Likely no widow's peak	Yep

Health
190. posted 8 Mar 2019, 17:52

Traits is pointless, (if slightly interesting), and you certainly don't use 23andme for ancestry purposes. The only point is the health tests and I said I didn't want to know about Parkinsons & Alzheimers anyway. I did say yes to the two cancer variants they look at and I don't have those. (Being a smoker is a far greater risk even if I had the variant) The only thing I have a slight variant for is Coeliac which I obviously don't have as I live on bread.

Health Predisposition

Age-Related Macular Degeneration Variant detected, not likely at increased risk
Alpha-1 Antitrypsin Deficiency Variant detected, not likely at risk
Celiac Disease Slightly increased risk
Familial HypercholesterolemiaNew Variants not detected
BRCA1/BRCA2 (Selected Variants) Variants not detected
G6PD Deficiency Variant not detected
Hereditary Hemochromatosis (HFE-Related) Variants not detected
Hereditary Thrombophilia Variants not detected

Keep in mind that while our Carrier Status reports cover many Variants, they don't include all possible Variants associated with each condition. So it's still possible to be a carrier of a Variant not included in our test.

Limb-Girdle Muscular Dystrophy Type 2D Variant detected
ARSACS Variant not detected
Agenesis of the Corpus Callosum with Peripheral Neuropathy Variant not detected
Autosomal Recessive Polycystic Kidney Disease Variant not detected
Beta Thalassemia and Related Hemoglobinopathies Variant not detected
Bloom Syndrome Variant not detected
Canavan Disease Variant not detected
Congenital Disorder of Glycosylation Type 1a (PMM2-CDG) Variant not detected
Cystic Fibrosis Variant not detected
D-Bifunctional Protein Deficiency Variant not detected
Dihydrolipoamide Dehydrogenase Deficiency Variant not detected
Familial Dysautonomia Variant not detected
Familial Hyperinsulinism (ABCC8-Related) Variant not detected
Familial Mediterranean Fever Variant not detected
Fanconi Anemia Group C Variant not detected
GRACILE Syndrome Variant not detected
Gaucher Disease Type 1 Variant not detected
Glycogen Storage Disease Type Ia Variant not detected
Glycogen Storage Disease Type Ib Variant not detected
Hereditary Fructose Intolerance Variant not detected
Herlitz Junctional Epidermolysis Bullosa (LAMB3-Related) Variant not detected
Leigh Syndrome, French Canadian Type Variant not detected
Limb-Girdle Muscular Dystrophy Type 2E Variant not detected
Limb-Girdle Muscular Dystrophy Type 2I Variant not detected

Maple Syrup Urine Disease Type 1B Variant not detected

Mucolipidosis Type IV Variant not detected

Neuronal Ceroid Lipofuscinosis (CLN5-Related) Variant not detected

Neuronal Ceroid Lipofuscinosis (PPT1-Related) Variant not detected

Niemann-Pick Disease Type A Variant not detected

Nijmegen Breakage Syndrome Variant not detected

Nonsyndromic Hearing Loss and Deafness, DFNB1 (GJB2-Related) Variant not detected

Pendred Syndrome and DFNB4 Hearing Loss (SLC26A4-Related) Variant not detected

Phenylketonuria and Related Disorders Variant not detected

Primary Hyperoxaluria Type 2 Variant not detected

Rhizomelic Chondrodysplasia Punctata Type 1 Variant not detected

Salla Disease Variant not detected

Sickle Cell Anemia Variant not detected

Sjögren-Larsson Syndrome Variant not detected

Tay-Sachs Disease Variant not detected

Tyrosinemia Type I Variant not detected

Usher Syndrome Type 1F Variant not detected

Usher Syndrome Type 3A Variant not detected

Zellweger Syndrome Spectrum (PEX1-Related) Variant not detected

PMDD
191. posted 10 Mar 2019, 13:50

"What is PMDD?

Premenstrual Dysphoric Disorder (also known as Premenstrual Dysphoria, Late Luteal Phase Dysphoric Disorder, or PMDD) is a cyclical, hormone-based mood disorder with symptoms arising during the premenstrual, or the luteal phase of the menstrual cycle and lasting until the onset of menstrual flow. It affects an estimated 5-10% of women of reproductive age. While PMDD is directly connected to the menstrual cycle, it is not a hormone imbalance. PMDD is a severe negative reaction to the natural rise and fall of estrogen and progesterone. It is a suspected genetic disorder with symptoms often worsening over time and around reproductive events including menarche, ovulation, pregnancy, birth, miscarriage, and menopause. Women with PMDD are at an increased risk for postpartum depression and suicidal behavior.

Symptoms of PMDD

Feelings of sadness or despair or even thoughts of suicide
    Feelings of tension or anxiety
    Panic attacks, mood swings, or frequent crying
    Lasting irritability or anger that affects other people
    Lack of interest in daily activities and relationships
    Trouble thinking or focusing
    Tiredness or low-energy
    Food cravings or binge eating
    Trouble sleeping
    Feeling out of control
    Physical symptoms, such as bloating, breast tenderness, headaches, and joint or muscle pain

PMS & PMDD

The term premenstrual syndrome (PMS) has a long history both clinical and colloquial. PMS is often used in the general population and popular culture in a way to explain or dismiss a woman's volatile mood, depression, anger, or behavior. Clinically, PMS is a collection of emotional and/or physical symptoms including bloating, breast tenderness, increased hunger, weepiness, and irritability. A woman or AFAB individual with PMS will have fewer, and usually less severe, premenstrual symptoms than a woman with PMDD.11 PMS is more common than PMDD, and as many as 80% of women experience some form of PMS in the second half of their menstrual cycle. Women may experience mild, moderate, or severe symptoms of PMS

PMS may interfere with a woman's quality of life, interpersonal relationships, or ability to attend work or school, according to the American College of Obstetricians and Gynecologists. However, PMS symptoms are generally more easily managed than PMDD and do not require prescription medication including antidepressants. PMS is also not classified as a mental illness in the Diagnostic and Statistical Manual of Mental Disorders, 5th Edition (DSM-5), while PMDD is.

PMDD is characterized by a cluster of mood symptoms that recur in the luteal phase of most menstrual cycles over the course of a year. An estimated 2-8% of women meet the criteria for PMDD. PMDD may be mild, moderate, or severe. PMDD is the only form of premenstrual disorder currently classified in the DSM-V. While PMS and PMDD are often used interchangeably in mainstream media and popular culture, the etiology, diagnosis, and treatment widely differ. It is important to use the correct terminology when discussing PMDD so that awareness, education, and treatment may be correctly achieved.

The Personal Impact of PMDD

PMDD can cause severe emotional, professional, and personal harm to those who have it. Sufferers of PMDD report damaging and impulsive behaviors that may include suddenly leaving a job or a relationship. Others report sudden and increased thoughts about suicide and self-harm. PMDD can feel like a "half-life". PMDD can feel like "one week of hell and three weeks of cleaning up". As women today have an estimated 450 periods during their lifetime, PMDD is a long term diagnosis. Providing sufferers with compassion and understanding is the first step in improving patient outcomes. The free tools, resources, information, and support provided by IAPMD can help you in this journey."

https://iapmd.org/about-pmdd

Joseph Confirmed
192. posted 10 Mar 2019, 20:52

Finally! A DNA match on the Paterson line. As I already had Stanley Charles Paterson in my tree, I don't think it matters that I post such a close relationship up although biologically we are really distant:-

    Predicted relationship: Distant Cousins
    Possible range: 5th - 8th cousins
    Confidence: Moderate

    5th–8th Cousin
    Shared DNA: 9 cM across 1 segments

DNA Match
2nd cousin 1x removed
Stanley Charles Paterson (1922 - 1983)
Grandfather of DNA Match
Charles Leonard Paterson (1897 - 1975)
Father of Stanley Charles Paterson
Joseph Charles Paterson (1854 - 1920)
Father of Charles Leonard Paterson
Stanley Thomas King Paterson (1901 - 1968)
Son of Joseph Charles Paterson

Next Two Days
193. posted 13 Mar 2019, 06:50

I have a very different attitude to news (specifically politics) to my husband. He loves watching/listening to debates for hours and is also very obsessed with American politics. I just go to BBC News and see the headline. Yesterday was the second Brexit vote and of course it was not agreed. Today they vote on No Deal and tomorrow they vote on extending Article 50. Fingers crossed No Deal is rejected and that there is an extension (that the EU agrees). Not quite sure what would be the benefit of an extension, not as if EU will change their current deal. It's either going to be a referendum or a general election. General election is pointless as I have mentioned many times before because both Labour & Torys don't have any solution to this problem. Referendum won't help as the last two years have polarised people even more.

Tee
194. posted 13 Mar 2019, 07:36

Thrulines has given this potential but as the match does not have a complete tree, I am assuming I have the correct Thomas

3rd cousin 1x removed
16cm 1 segment

DNA Match
3rd cousin 1x removed of son
Thomas Henry Tee (1901 -)
Probably Grandfather of DNA Match
George Henry Tee (1870 -)
Father of Thomas Henry Tee
William Tee (1830 - 1905)
Father of George Henry Tee
Jessie Tee (1868 -)
Daughter of William Tee

Non Binding
195. posted 13 Mar 2019, 20:30

MPs reject a no deal Brexit by 312 to 308 in a non binding vote. Basically up to EU. Next vote tomorrow.

Labour Abstain
196. posted 14 Mar 2019, 17:32

Flipping hate political parties. Times like this it should be a free vote. Anyway, an amendment calling for a 2nd referendum has been rejected, 334 to 85. If my 'bubble' was anything to go by, it should have been the other way round.

Delay
197. posted 14 Mar 2019, 19:02

So it continues to drag on, nigh on 3 years since the referendum and MPs vote 412 to 202 for Brexit to be delayed beyond 29 March. I expect the EU will grant one. "The EU Commission says it will "take note" of tonight's votes but that a request for an extension of Article 50 will require the unanimous agreement of all 27 member states."

Also, from the earlier vote *"MPs have voted against the Labour Party's frontbench amendment, which rejects the prime minister's deal, no-deal and calls for an extension of*

Article 50 to allow time to find a different approach, by 318 votes to 302 - a majority of 16."

Rock Paper Scissors
198. posted 15 Mar 2019, 07:01

Just noticed 14 days til 29th

Sympathy for May getting on with a difficult job has run out. If we can't have another vote on something that was so close, why can she have a third vote on something that was so drastically lost twice before? I know I don't truly understand the 'backstop' but whatever is bugging people about it, their view won't have changed. And its ONLY THE TRANSITION FFS.

Got emails/facebook feed from Lib Dems over the last few days calling for another referendum. That is not going to happen, stop flogging a dead horse. Might have to stop my subs to them, they have not helped.

Christian Paton
199. posted 16 Mar 2019, 18:03

I was just going through my sons hints to assign my side/his fathers side groups. I wanted to ensure I had all of his fathers side done. Went off on a tangent when I got to one match.   Only 6cm on 1 segment but a match nonetheless.

The thing about Christian Paton is that she is the mother of Jean Mustart who we thought might be Alexander Patersons mother.

This matches tree is set to private so I have sent a message requesting access. Fingers crossed!

My daughter has the same match but bizarrely my nephew and I don't.

176

Alloa
200. posted 16 Mar 2019, 21:18

"In 1887, John Bartholomew's Gazetteer of the British Isles described Alloa like this:

Alloa, par. and seaport and chief town of Clackmannansh., on N. bank of river Forth, 6½ m. E. of Stirling by rail, 5502 ac., pop. 11,638; town, pop. 8822; 5 Banks, 3 newspapers. Market-days, Wednesday and Saturday. Has a good harb., wet and dry dock; there are breweries and distilleries, and the mfr. of glass, woollens, machinery, and pottery, is carried on; while in the vicinity are extensive coal-pits. (For shipping statistics, see Appendix.) Adjacent to the town are Alloa House (seat of Earl of Mar and Kerrie) and the remains of ancient mansion of Earls of Mar."

http://www.visionofbritain.org.uk/place/17120

Match responded so I think we have a real confirmation that Jean Mustart is the mother of Alexander Paterson. I had 54 people in a workings tree and I shall be adding them and more based on this match. I hope this means I have lots of cousin stories to write up. This is a real bonus of the new layout that Ancestry has. If I hadn't gone through the new feature of common ancestors I would never have found this.

> Predicted relationship: Distant Cousins (to son & daughter)
> Possible range: 5th - 8th cousins
> Confidence: Moderate
> Shared DNA: 6 cM across 1 segments
>
> DNA Match
> **5th cousin** to me but NOT a match to me (5th cousin 1x removed to son & daughter & the other Mustart contact)
> Thomas Yorke (1889 - 1969)
> Grandfather of DNA Match
> Edith Matilda Mustart (1867 - 1932)
> Mother of Thomas Yorke
> Robert Mustart (1837 - 1913)
> Father of Edith Matilda Mustart
> Robert Mustart (1788 - 1868)
> Father of Robert Mustart
> **Alexander Mustart (1765 -)**

Father of Robert Mustart
Jean Mustart (1792 -)
Daughter of Alexander Mustart
Alexander Paterson (1825 - 1865)
Son of Jean Mustart
Joseph Charles Paterson (1854 - 1920)
Son of Alexander Paterson

James King
201. posted 17 Mar 2019, 09:41

Boy had another match on my side that I don't have:-

Predicted Relationship: Distant Cousin to son
Amount of shared DNA is 6 centimorgans across 1 DNA segments

DNA Match
5th cousin to me
Ethel Caroline Boulting (1895 -)
Grandmother of DNA Match
William Boulting (1866 -)
Father of Ethel Caroline Boulting
Elizabeth King (1842 -)
Mother of William Boulting
John King (1806 -)
Father of Elizabeth King
James King (1768 - 1861)
Father of John King
Joseph King (1802 - 1838)
Son of James King
John King (1830 - 1888)
Son of Joseph King

I had 1806 John King in my tree (with hints) but not his daughter Elizabeth
so that is all new from match.

Trayton Geall

Trayton Geall was born in 1822, his parents were Thomas Geall and Elizabeth Funnell. He wasn't baptised until his sister Harriet was, on the 14th March 1824. Trayton was an ag lab. He married Mary Hallett in 1845 and they had at least 6 children. Trayton died in Ripe on the 10th September 1876 and was buried at the graveyard of St John the Baptist church.

This man is very ordinary, his life is like 80% of my tree. I wouldn't normally write his story up but I stood on his grave today.

I am currently distracted by a Seth Geall/Berry so I will write up more about Trayton tomorrow.

As an aside, on my drive to Sussex today I noticed a few houses flying a flag that was blue with yellow birds on it. It turns out it is the flag of Sussex - how bizarre!

https://en.m.wikipedia.org/wiki/Flag_of_Sussex

Harriet Cornwall
203. posted 17 Mar 2019, 22:15

Harriet Cornwall was born c1809 and baptised at the Parish Church of Benenden, Kent when she was 6 on the 29th October 1815. She married Richard Berry on the 25th November 1832 in Heathfield and they had at least 5 children before he died c1842. Or did he die c1850?

Harriet had at least 3 more children between these dates but according to the 1851 census, the children are all Geall, not Berry. Harriet married Thomas Geall on the 13th November 1852 in Ripe. This date is after the birth of the children and the 1851 census. In 1861, her son Seth Berry uses his correct surname on the census whereas he used Geall in 1851. His (half?) siblings still use Geall in 1861.

Harriet and Thomas have at least 3 more children of their own after 1852. Thomas Geall dies in 1864. (He had at least 5 children from his previous marriage to Elizabeth Funnell) Harriet remarried again on the 1st August

1866 in Berwick to George Russell (also previously married with children).
George must have died c1885 as Harriet is a widow in the 1891 census and
there is no trace of her after that.

I am aware that until now, I have not mentioned the 50 people killed by a
right wing lunatic a few days ago in Christchurch, New Zealand.   Truly
horrific and like all terrorist activity, totally incomprehensible.

St John the Baptist Ripe
204. posted 18 Mar 2019, 07:53

When I entered exact death dates into Ancestry, hints came up for 'findagrave'
so I have uploaded my gravestone pics to there.

    Henry Geall *https://www.findagrave.com/memorial/187150573*
    Trayton Geall *https://www.findagrave.com/memorial/187150560*

Unfortunately there were stinging nettles on bottom of that stone so cannot
transcribe all of it but:-

        In affectionate
        Remembrance of
        TRAYTON GEALL.
        Who died Sept. 10th 1876.
        Aged 54 Years
        And HENRY GEALL,
        Who Died ?? 3rd 1877
        Aged ?? Years

        ??? be done
        ??? XXI? (stinging nettles)

    Mary Hallett *https://www.findagrave.com/memorial/187150591*

        In loving
180

Memory of
MARY GEALL,
Widow of
TRAYTON GEALL.
Who died July 6th. 1891,
Aged 66 Years.

Not gone from memory, not gone from love
But gone to our fathers home above

Martha Geall *https://www.findagrave.com/memorial/187150583*

Her sister Mary doesn't currently have a page on this site. It's a bit weird why she is on this stone as she was married (so surname Tappenden) and she appears to have died in East Grinstead.

In Memory of
MARTHA
Daughter of TRAYTON and
MARY GEALL.
Died June 30th 1898.
Aged 43 Years.

A light is from our household gone,
The voice we loved is stilled,
The place is vacant in our home,
Which never can be filled,

Also of MARY,
Their eldest daughter,
Died June 12th 1902,
Aged 57 Years.

I am surprised at the punctuation on these 3 stones as I thought every mark cost something. (lower case was actually caps but used lower to differentiate size)

Chalvington & Ripe
205. posted 18 Mar 2019, 09:27

It turns out I have been thinking of going to these villages for 6 years now!
Time flies!

https://sites.google.com/site/theashleaze/genealogy/research-blog/ripe

https://sites.google.com/site/theashleaze/genealogy/research-blog/alfristonrd

I have driven past the signs to Ripe several times over this period, when we go to Eastbourne or anywhere down there (and we go for caravan weekends down the South Coast a few times a year usually), and each time I see the signs I think, shall I do a detour? But then think I really need a day for it and drive past.

I didn't really go with a plan apart from looking up what pubs there were. I just thought I would wander around the graveyards and see if I could recognise any names. To be fair, I didn't actually expect to see any gravestones as they were ag labs therefore too poor plus they were non conformists so they went to meeting halls rather than churches. I was secretly hoping the pub would have something about The Onion Pie Murders.

I sort of arrived in The Street (Ripe) by accident and parked up. Couldn't see where the pub was supposed to be. Wandered up the road to see if I could find it and found St John the Baptist church. The first gravestones were illegible and I was thinking it was a waste of time, the legible ones were all to recent to be of any use to me. I then found 3 with the name Trayton Geall on. I knew from the dates and names these people were not direct ancestors but something about Trayton rang a bell and they were Geall so I took some pictures. I didn't try to get in the church, it looked closed. I found out last night that a Leonard Trayton Geall has a memorial plaque in there.

I then went back to the car. I sort of imagined that Chalvington & Ripe were like Fylingdales/Robin Hoods Bay where they are considered the same place but actually easier to drive between. (I also found the pub - it was mostly knocked down with the site being made into houses) But the signs for Chalvington took me back to Ripe. I then saw a no through road for Chalvington Church on Church Farm Lane so parked up and went down the road. I ended up at St Bartholomews Church which was definitely closed but

182

is on a public footpath so you could go through the graveyard. It is a very small pretty church and apparently parts of it date back to 1100! Nothing of note in that graveyard.

Strolling back to car I noticed the village hall. So if I had turned right after St John the Baptist in Ripe, I would have been at St Bartholomews in Chalvington. Chalvington & Ripe really are the same place! I do not understand why they have different road signs. It is just two small roads. The roads are very pretty and several houses were very old and would definitely say my ancestors saw those buildings too.

I was hungry so decided to find somewhere to eat and found the only place in the area, again by accident, the Yew Tree pub. After some cheesy chips I decided to go to Alfriston. Drove through Berwick again!

Alfriston is very old. Signs on the pubs; Star Inn rebuilt early 16th century. The George Inn - first transfer of innkeepers license - 1397!; The Steamer Inn dating from the 15th century... So my ancestors probably drunk in them.

I was heading towards St Andrews church when I saw a National Trust place, the Clergy House, being a member I popped in. I then went to the church. St Andrews possibly had some Lower stones but they were illegible and my camera battery had run out. This church was open to visitors but I didn't go in as I was worried about my car park ticket running out. Walking back I found the 1801 Congregational Church. It seemed to have an event (service? it was a Sunday) so I didn't go in but this is where my ancestors would be if they are anywhere. It was a United Reformed Church but I didn't get a pic of the plaque next to it. (phone out of memory too!)

When I got home, I found that Trayton Geall was indeed already in my tree. Martha had a photo hint of her gravestone too.

It was a nice day out, I need to go to Alfriston again to check out the United Reformed Church. There are other villages that still need looking at in that area too. Maybe sooner than 6 years this time.

Richard Berry
206. posted 18 Mar 2019, 13:03

Harriet Cornwall continues to puzzle. She also seems to have chased Richard for some form of child support (or more likely the Poor Law Union did) back in 1823 but that date does appear to be incorrect by about 10 years:-

Catalogue description Bastardy examination

Reference: PAR372/34/1/3
Title: Bastardy examination
Description: Harriet Cornwall charges Richard Berry of Framfield
Date: 30 Oct 1823
Held by: East Sussex Record Office
Former reference in its original department: PAR372/34/1/3
                Lan

http://discovery.nationalarchives.gov.uk/details/r/7f1bcb80-57ec-4950-ae1b-0eb7c0b2a78c

Anyway the detail is not available and they married 10 years later so I guess it was sorted?

Another Richard Berry of Mayfield rather than Framfield has two maintenance orders from an Ann Collins at the same sort of time, I don't think they are the same person.

EU
207. posted 21 Mar 2019, 06:44

Are *****. I know a couple of months extension is not going to resolve anything. But really annoyed and surprised the EU won't agree an extension unless the deal is backed. If the deal was backed we wouldn't need an extension.... ?!?

So 8 days left :(

Revoke Article 50
208. posted 23 Mar 2019, 19:37

So I did it. I went on the march requesting a people vote despite all of my other posts saying what's the point? Also 'signed' the online petition (now at over 4 million) to revoke Article 50. Another pointless gesture.

Brexit march: Hundreds of thousands join referendum protest

James Paterson
209. posted 24 Mar 2019, 09:23

Confirming the Jean Mustart connection means in theory I could go back on Charles but we still know nothing about him. All we know is Charles Paterson married Jean Mustart on the 14th December 1818 in Stirling.

Charles could be born in Stirling c1792 or he could have been born anywhere else in the world. Another option was he was born in Alloa like Jean was.

On familysearch we have some possibles:-

Paterson (no first name) - St Ninians, Stirling 4/9/1791 parents Alexander Paterson & Helen Steven
Paterson (no first name) - St Ninians, Stirling 16/8/1793 parent Alexander Paterson
Paterson (no first name) - Alloa, Clackmannan 19/7/1794 parents James Paterson & Margaret Snadan

I think Paterson (no first name) - Alloa, Clackmannan 22/7/1800 parents James Paterson & Margaret Snadan, would be too late.

I like Alexander Paterson as Charles called his son Alexander but I really think I shall have to keep the tree ending with Charles.

Robert Paterson
210. posted 24 Mar 2019, 18:26

Someone contacted me as they had a Thru Lines hint from my tree for a Robert Paterson. This confused me somewhat as I have no Robert Paterson in my tree. Turns out that Thru Lines made a connection between one of my workings trees. It was back from 2016 when I tried to find all St Ninians Patersons.

This is confirmation that Thru Lines can be as much nonsense as the 'potential ancestor' hints. I know this because I have looked at their tree and they are from Campsie, not St Nin.

However, back in 2016 I stopped working on this tree due to lack of free data (being Scotland). Ancestry now has a lot more Scottish info so I am going to revisit this tree. This tree currently has 380 people with 883 hints so it should keep me busy for a while.

Another Mustart
211. posted 25 Mar 2019, 08:02

Did go through quite a lot of those hints but in the end decided it was pointless. What was good was my 'F' numbering system which meant it was easy to find the relevant post on here to see what I had already done.

Today I thought I should go through nephews matches with common ancestors just to see if there was anything non Barber. And there is! He has a Christian Paton match that us 3 don't. I think this definitely confirms Mustart is right now. I had put off adding the cousins but I can do that now.

Predicted Relationship: Distant Cousin (4th cousin 2x removed to nephew)

Amount of shared DNA is 7 centimorgans across 1 DNA segments

DNA Match
4th cousin 1x removed to me
Janet Hutchison (1878 -)
Grandmother of DNA Match
Robert Hutchison (1823 -)
Father of Janet Hutchison
Mary Mustart (1797 -)
Mother of Robert Hutchison
Alexander Mustart (1765 -)

Father of Mary Mustart
Jean Mustart (1792 -)
Daughter of Alexander Mustart
Alexander Paterson (1825 - 1865)
Son of Jean Mustart
Joseph Charles Paterson (1854 - 1920)
Son of Alexander Paterson

Invasion of Martinique
212. posted 25 Mar 2019, 12:16

Robert Mustart was born on the 17th October 1788, in Alloa, son of Alexander Mustart and Christian Paton. He was baptised on the 20th October 1788.

On the 7th September 1896, at the age of 17, Robert joined the Royal Navy. The first ship he served on was HMS Forester.

https://en.wikipedia.org/wiki/HMS_Forester_(1806)

By 1809, he was on HMS Recruit, he is ranked as a "carpenter" rather than a seaman or any of the usual ranks. Robert received the Martinique Clasp on the 17th June 1809 for his part in the Invasion of Martinique.

"...Following repairs, Recruit participated in the invasion of Martinique in January 1809. Napier observed that Fort Edward at Fort Royal Bay appeared abandoned. He took a gig and with four men, landed, scaled the fort's walls, and hoisted a British flag. Sir Alexander Cochrane immediately landed marines to occupy the fort and turn its mortars, which had not been spiked, against the French.[6] In 1847 the Admiralty authorized the issuance of the Naval General Service Medal with clasp "Martinique" to all survivors of the campaign...."

https://en.wikipedia.org/wiki/HMS_Recruit_(1806)

https://en.wikipedia.org/wiki/Invasion_of_Martinique_(1809)

On the 12th March 1810, Robert was in Portsmouth and he married Elizabeth Anne Childs at St Thomas' and they went on to have at least one daughter. Elizabeth died in 1833 and was buried in Chatham on the 4th June.

On the 23rd September 1835, Robert left the Navy, the last ship he served on appears to be the HMS Anson but cannot find a wiki entry for an Anson that was in service around that time. Robert appears to have remarried to an Eliza c1836 but I can't find a wedding doc. Robert and Eliza have at least 4 children. He does not appear to have worked after leaving the Navy, in 1851 he is described as a 'Pensioned Cap'n of RN' and in 1861 he is a 'Warrant Officer - retired'. I have not seen any document saying he was a Captain, just a carpenter.

Robert died in Chatham in 1868.

Admiralty Clerk
213. posted 25 Mar 2019, 13:21

Robert Mustart (Jnr) was baptised in Chatham at St Marys on the 2nd October 1836. His life wasn't as interesting as his fathers but he had a career which is slightly different to normal so lets write him up.

In 1836 he married Amelia Elizabeth Bishop and they went on to have at least 12 children. (The 1911 census says 14 children, 11 children survived and 3 died - have to find the other 2) In 1861 he was working as a schoolmaster. In 1871 his occupation is a very long sentence but apart from the word schoolmaster is illegible. Want to know what it says!! By 1881 he has had a change and is now a clerk to a builder. In 1891 another change in role; civil service clerk. Robert then retires and in 1901 is described as a retired civil service clerk but in 1911 he is listed as "Pensioned 2nd Div Clerk Admiralty Office" so it has to be assumed that is who he was working for in the 1890s.

Robert died on the 2nd May 1913. He was living at 84 Crescent Rd, Wood Green when he died and he left £122 9s to his son Leonard Mustart.

Lunatic

Phoebe Mustart was baptised on the 5th June 1872 at St Johns in Deptford. She lived with her family until at least 1881 but she is not with them in 1891 when there is no trace of her. On the 26th January 1899, Phoebe was admitted to Essex County Lunatic Asylum. She was discharged later that year on the 28th September and her discharge tick is in the 'recovered' box. However she went in again on the 17th February 1900, this time staying there for 10 years. (1901 census lunatic box has a squiggle in it so not sure which of the 4 categories applies). On the 3rd May 1910 she was discharged, again marked as recovered. Later that month, on the 31st May 1910, Phoebe was admitted to the Middlesex County Asylum in Upper Tooting. In the 1911 census she was still there and marked as a lunatic. On the 6th June 1912, she was discharged from that asylum and moved to one in Essex. Phoebe appears to have remained at this institution for 12 years until her death on the 6th June 1924.

Yorke

215. posted 26 Mar 2019, 07:29

Harry Frederick Yorke was baptised in Barby, Northhamptonshire on the 25th April 1852. At some point he moved to London. He was married by 1875 as that is when his daughter Adelaide was born. Not sure of his wifes name - options are Violet May Birch, Agnes Maria Braybrooke or Alice Jukes. Whoever she was, she died (during?) after their son Frederick Headley Yorke was born in 1877.

On the 7th April 1887, Harry remarried in Wandsworth to Edith Matilda Mustart. Harry & Edith had at least 8 children together.

Ediths youngest sister was Agnes. Agnes Mustart married Frederick Headley Yorke. At first I thought Agnes married her nephew! However it is her 'Step Nephew' which isn't a thing so it is ok. Their marriage was in Canada despite both of them coming from South London.

Hawaii

Maria Mustart was born in Chatham in 1843. She married John Bush in 1869 and they went on to have at least 8 children. Maria and John were living in Gillingham in 1881 and John was working as a school master. After that their life gets a bit vague. In 1891, Maria is living in Chatham but John isn't there. I think he might have been in Hawaii. At least 3 of their children ended up in Hawaii and one has an arrival date of 1884. There is no trace of Maria after the 1891 census so she presumably joined her husband in Hawaii.

Maria & John both died in Honolulu in 1929.

Tasmania
217. posted 26 Mar 2019, 11:59

Christian Hutchison was born on the 17th May 1819 in Alloa. On the 13th June 1846 she married William Fair in Alva. William was a shoemaker employing 2 men. William and Christian had at least 2 children. On the 28th July 1855, the family arrived at Hobart, Tasmania. As there doesn't appear to be a criminal record and the arrival document doesn't relate to criminals, I can only assume they emigrated there. There was a Launceston Immigration Aid Society at the time which might have paid for their trip.

They had another daughter in 1857. Christian died in Launceston in 1860.

Middle Names
218. posted 27 Mar 2019, 07:42

William Laing was born on the 2nd July 1857 in Stirling. His parents were Alexander Laing and Rachel Paterson.

Mary Ann Mackie was born in St Ninians c1861. Her parents were William Goodwin Mackie and Anne McLeod.

William and Mary had at least 5 children and 4 have grandparent middle names. Not unusual too see a maternal surname as a middle name on one of the children but unusual to see all of them have it (the 5th has Cairns - must be a reason for that?)

Alexander Paterson Laing
William Mackie Laing
Robert McLeod Laing
Annie McLeod Laing
Frederick Cairns Laing

Pneumonia
219. posted 27 Mar 2019, 18:34

Robert Manning was born in Swansea on the 18th January 1887. By 1901, the family is back in Essex. Robert is working as an office boy. On the 2nd January 1904, Robert joined the Navy. He was initially on HMS Northampton but he went on lots of other ships such as HMS Pembroke (which ones??), HMS Hibernia, HMS Vindictive, HMS London, HMS Scylla and a few I can't read. He appears to have been on Hibernia and Pembroke during WW1 so not sure if he saw action. Dates do not seem to tie into anything specific on the wiki page:-
https://en.wikipedia.org/wiki/HMS_Hibernia_(1905)

On the 17th March 1913 (I think), he was promoted to Able Seaman. Robert was also promoted to Leading Seaman and then Petty Officer (non commissioned) but again not sure of the dates.

Robert was still serving in the Navy on Pembroke 1 in Chatham when he contracted flu. The flu turned into pneumonia and he died on the 28th February 1920. He was buried in Chingford Cemetery in Essex on the 5th March 1920.

Manitoba Coop
220. posted 27 Mar 2019, 19:58

Thomas Yorke was born in Wandsworth on the 1st January 1889. He was baptised at St Annes on the 24th February. Thomas lived with his family in Wandsworth until at least 1901. On the 16th August 1906, aged just 17, Thomas emigrated to Canada on the Canada. His occupation is given as clerk.

There is another possible arrival in 1911, he may have gone back to the UK for a visit. Thomas married Winifred Annie Longstaff on the 12th June 1937 in Brandon, Manitoba. They went on to have 3 children. Thomas died in Brandon on the 20th May 1969.

Nothing out of the ordinary here and I wouldn't normally type this up (especially as a 'recent' death) but he has an obituary in the Brandon Sun on the 21st May 1969 (got that out quick!) and I thought I would transcribe it. I think it is ok to type something up that relates to living people if it is already in the public domain?

"Thomas Yorke

The death of Thomas Yorke, 80, of 41 Whillier Drive, occured in the city on Tuesday. Mr Yorke was born in London, England and came to Canada in 1906, settling in Moline. He served overseas in the First World War and following the war returned to Moline where he was employed by the Manitoba Coop, later taking up farming.

Since 1941, Mr Yorke has resided in Brandon. Surviving are his wife, Winifred; a son, Keith of Brandon; and two daughters, Joan in Geneva; and Mrs Stanley Thickens (Phyllis) of Brandon. There are two grandchildren. Thomas and Roseanne Yorke. Three brothers and two sisters also survive. Archie and Leonard in England. Harry White Rock BC; Constance and Stella, also residing in England.

Funeral service will be held at St Matthews Anglican Cathedral on Friday at 2pm. Internment will follow in Brandon cemetery. The Very Rev. T. W. Wilkinson will officiate. Arrangements are with Brockie Donovan."

29th March 2019
221. posted 29 Mar 2019, 07:39

I don't know what's going on.

I think they are having a 3rd vote today, if agreed there is extension to 22nd May (what for?)

Sigh.

12ᵗʰ April
222. posted 31 Mar 2019, 17:13

What next?

Monday, 1 April: MPs hold another set of votes on Brexit options to see if they can agree on a way forward
Wednesday, 3 April: Potentially another round of so-called "indicative votes"
Wednesday, 10 April: Emergency summit of EU leaders to consider any UK request for further extension
Friday, 12 April: Brexit day, if UK does not seek/EU does not grant further delay
23-26 May: European Parliamentary elections

(from BBC news)

I hope it does not drag onto the elections - that would be a waste of time and money if we are leaving. (Of course I want elections as I don't want to leave but y'know what I mean)

In the much more interesting world of ancestry, somebody contacted me asking to see my tree as their wife was a distant DNA match with my Mum. In a weird turn of events, this person worked out the connection! (I wasn't in an investigative mood to work it out myself when they gave me access to their tree, there were lots of Sussex surnames and I dreaded it being another Thomas Barber.)

> Predicted relationship: Distant Cousins to Mum
> Possible range: 5th - 8th cousins
> Confidence: Moderate
>
> DNA match
> **6th cousin 2x removed** to Me
> Edward Manser (1896 -)
> Grandfather of DNA Match
> George Alfred Manser (1869 -)
> Father of Edward Manser

Alfred Colyer Manser (1848 -)
Father of George Alfred Manser
Francis Manser
Father of Alfred Colyer Manser
Thomas Manser (1752 -)
Father of Francis Manser
Edward Manser (1708 -)
Father of Thomas Manser
Susannah Manser (1738 - 1787)
Daughter of Edward Manser
Thomas Hoad (1772 - 1838)
Son of Susannah Manser
Sarah Hoad (1796 - 1838)
Daughter of Thomas Hoad
Eleanor Barber (1825 - 1867)
Daughter of Sarah Hoad

I have some dates of the new people to add still. I had Thomas Manser in my tree but all of his descendants are copied from the match. First time Edward Manser has been verified and cool to be able to do so as he is a 7th Gt Grandfather.

63
223. posted 31 Mar 2019, 19:55

Mum finally has shared ancestor hints. 63 of them!! That's this evening sorted - how many will be Barber? how many will I already have that aren't Barber?

Undecided
224. posted 1 Apr 2019, 08:27

I quite often get this and just leave the person blank but as I am sort of checking my workings against two public trees, I sort of want to go with their 'answer'.

Elizabeth Hutchison was born in Alloa on the 4th June 1815 and baptised there on the 13th June. Her parents were Michael Hutchison and Mary Mustart. That is all I know.

As I say, would normally leave it at that. There is a hint that she married a Henry Anderson in Fife on the 24th May 1834. They have 4 children by the 1841 census. Some of the public trees have this (not that that is any indication it is right) but my two trees have her marrying John Carmichael. The argument for this marriage is that the 1851, 1861, 1871 census have correct birth place. Argument against - where is she in 1841 and where is the marriage doc?

I am going with Carmichael.

Feus Brewery
225. posted 1 Apr 2019, 17:59

John Carmichael was born c1817 in Tullibody which is about 3 miles outside Alloa. In 1841 he was possibly working as a ploughman in Alloa. On the 20th November 1843, he married Elizabeth Hutchison (Hutcheson on doc which is why couldn't find on earlier post), in Alloa. John and Elizabeth went on to have at least 9 children.

In 1851, they were living at 'Bothy' in Alloa and John was working as a brewer. By 1861 they had moved to 18 Upper Bdge St in Stirling and Michael is an ale brewer. There is no trace of the family in 1871. I assume they are in the process of moving to Auchterarder in Perthshire.

"In 1887, John Bartholomew's Gazetteer of the British Isles described Auchterarder like this:

Auchterarder, par. and market town, SE. Perthsh., 14 miles SW. of Perth by rail -- par., 11,181 ac., pop. 3648; town, pop. 2666; P.O., T.O., 2 Banks.Market-day, Saturday. A. Castle and A. House are in vicinity."

http://www.visionofbritain.org.uk/place/16908

John had 21 documents on the Perthshire, Scotland, Cess, Stent and Valuation Rolls, 1650-1899 between 1872 and 1894. (There might be more if there aren't any other John Carmichaels in Auchterarder). In 1872 they show him as being the proprietor of a house and garden, a brewing premises and a large room and malting premises. The house is valued at £15, the brewing premises at £7 10s and the malting premises at £12 10s. These valuations did not change in the 22 years. He paid tax to Colonel Hunter of £3 1s 3d for a couple of years, then to Major Hunter and from 1888 onwards to James Reid. Again the tax did not change over that period.

It would appear that the brewery was called 'Feus':-

"The Feus Brewery was first recorded in the valuation rolls of 1858, when it was occupied by Robert Mailer and owned by his son, also Robert, a local solicitor. Robert senior was recorded as a brewer and maltster living in Feus in 1851, so it is likely that the Feus Brewery was in operation before 1858. The brewery was sold in 1861 for £300 (about £30,000 in today's money) to David Farquharson, a partner in Scott & Co.

After David was declared bankrupt in 1863 the brewery was offered for sale for £220 (about £22,000 in today's money), and it was purchased by John Young, a surgeon in Dunning. Scott & Co continued as tenants, but offered their brewing utensils for sale in 1864; they were still recorded as the tenants in 1869.

The brewery was briefly taken on by James Christie in 1869 following the dissolution of the partnership of J. & A. Christie.

John Carmichael bought the brewery in 1872 and he was the proprietor until 1893, trading as John Carmichael & Co. The brewery then passed to Carmichael & Co and was eventually acquired by Carmichael & Co Ltd in 1897, which renamed it as the Strathearn Brewery."

https://scottishbrewingheritage.org/buildings.php?p=592

It is not clear when John died. The last valuation doc is for the year 1894-95 and he was apparently trading to 1893. Public trees have a death of 3rd December 1893 but why would he have a valuation the next year? It can't be his son John as he stayed in Alloa and mades coaches.

Out of interest I thought I would look up the landlords and found this:-

"...Lieut.-Colonel James Hunter erected the mansion at Auchterarder. On his death in 1874 he left the estate to his nephew, Major Patrick Hunter, who, in 1887, sold it to the late Mr. James Reid, Lord Dean of Guild of Glasgow."

196

Jersey
226. posted 1 Apr 2019, 20:44

Henry Carmichael was born in Cambus, about 3 miles from Alloa on the 26th September 1844. By the age of 17, he had moved away from the family and was boarding at Dumfries New Church, his occupation is given as 'pupil teacher'. By 1871, he is the minister of Free Church, Manse in Peebles. The Reverend Henry Carmichael married Christian Hervey McClelland in Wigtown on the 11th January 1872. The Rev and Christian went on to have at least 5 children before he died on the 11th August 1879. He is buried at St Andrews Cemetery in Peebles. Henry left £903 17s 1d to his wife.

Then Christian goes to St Helier Jersey. Why? In 1881, she is living there at 5 Ocean View with her children, sister and servant. She is described as an annuitant so presumably was receiving a pension from the church. By 1891, they are back in Scotland, in Glasgow. In 1901, she moves down to Hornsey in Middlesex to live with her son Henry. Christian went back to Scotland as she died at Bridge of Allan on the 18th January 1929. She is buried at Logie Cemetery in Stirling. Her daughter Christian was the executor of her will, her estate was valued at £1,231 1s 4d.

Arlington
227. posted 4 Apr 2019, 19:22

Vera Adie Moore was born in New York City on the 1st December 1892. She lived in Manhattan with her family until at least 1905. Vera married Harrison Ray Weaver in Westchester on the 1st September 1915. They lived in Scarsdale and had at least 2 children. Vera died in Winter Park, Orange County, Florida on the 15th February 1994. She would have been 101 years old!!

I think this is only the 2nd person in my tree that had reached this grand old age. The other was Rose Florence Moxley.

So as I already had a post called '101', including a bit on her son in law, Lieutenant Theodore Thomas Edwards. He served in WW2. He died on the 23rd September 1990, in Orange, Florida but he was buried at Arlington Cemetery. I am sure I have seen other veterans buried at Arlington before now but don't seem to have done a post mentioning it if I did.

Achievers
228. posted 4 Apr 2019, 19:57

I appear to have zero Mustart/Paton DNA in me. Which is probably why I never achieve anything. The descendants of Alexander and Christian all seem to have trades or emigrate, no ag labs or servants. (There are a few but not to the extent of other lines)

Although it could be nurture rather than nature. If your father is a Reverend or a school master surely you are more likely to be successful?

Some examples

Michael Wotherspoon 1850-1895 Head Architect (father appears to have been a jack of all trades) 2nd cousin 3x removed

Dr Henry Carmichael 1872-1957 (father Reverend) 3rd cousin 2x removed

Lawrence Towers Carmichael 1876-1946 Colonial Produce Merchant (ditto father/relationship)

Alexander Paterson Laing 1889- Civil Engineer (father school teacher) 2nd cousin 2x removed

Reverend William Mackie Laing 1889-1968 (ditto)

2nd Lieutenant Robert McLeod Laing 1893-1916 (ditto)

Dr Frederick Cairns Laing 1901- (ditto)

198

I think these are my first architect and civil engineer. Definitely my first Colonial Produce Merchant.

Gatekeeper
229. posted 11 Apr 2019, 09:25

Another Hoad DNA match has made me go slightly off blood because despite what the census docs say, a couple of women had an occupation.

Fanny Stevens married John Simmons on the 16th June 1849. John was a plate layer for the railways. In June 1854, Fanny also got a job with London, Brighton & South Coast railways. She was the gatekeeper at Hailsham level crossing. Working as the gatekeeper means that you get the gatekeeper cottage next to the level crossing to live in. Fanny got 5s a week for being the gatekeeper but had 2s 6d deducted for the house. It would appear that unlike todays automatic crossings, the barrier was always down and the gatekeeper raised the barrier when somebody wants to cross the line.

Fanny and John had at least 8 children between 1849 and 1869. I suspect that Fanny was taken ill in early 1871. On the 17th May 1871, a temporary gatekeeper, Mitchell, was put in place at Hailsham. They earned the full 5 shillings indicating they were not renting the house. Fanny died on the 9th June 1871 and Mitchell stayed as the gatekeeper until the 27th June.

Then one of their children, Ellen, took over the role of gatekeeper. She was paid 2/6 as well indicating that Ellen took the job on to keep their house.

Ellen was the gatekeeper until at least the 31st December 1881. She married a signalman, William Levett (the blood connection), in 1883. Ellen and William had at least 3 children before she died in 1903. William remarried to Naomi Hunnisett in 1905 and they had at least a couple of children too. William was living at 47 Summerheath Rd, Hailsham when he died in January 1940. He left £562 9d to Arthur Levett and Alfred Baker.

Pelling Maddox
230. posted 11 Apr 2019, 20:13

Couple of new confirmations on husbands maternal side:-

Predicted Relationship: Distant Cousin
shared DNA is 11 centimorgans across 1 DNA segments

DNA Match
4th cousin 1x removed
Alice Ellen Parsons (1894 - 1978)
Grandmother of DNA Match
Alice Mary Sargant (1858 - 1902)
Mother of Alice Ellen Parsons
Caroline Pelling (1821 - 1884)
Mother of Alice Mary Sargant
Robert Pelling (1787 - 1861)
Father of Caroline Pelling
William Henry Pelling (1832 -)
Son of Robert Pelling
Emma Ruth Pelling (1864 - 1932)
Daughter of William Henry Pelling

Predicted Relationship: Distant Cousin
shared DNA is 11 centimorgans across 1 DNA segments

DNA Match
4th cousin
Winifred Moore (1906 -)
Grandmother of DNA Match
Samuel Ernest Moore (1870 - 1954)
Father of Winifred Moore
Amelia Maddox (1838 - 1896)
Mother of Samuel Ernest Moore
John William Maddox (1805 - 1878)
Father of Amelia Maddox
William Maddox (1847 - 1918)
Son of John William Maddox

Couple More
231. posted 13 Apr 2019, 21:27

One generation back for Mildenhall and one forward for Wadey:-

Predicted relationship: Distant Cousins
Possible range: 5th - 8th cousins
Confidence: Moderate
7cm 1 segment

DNA Match
5th cousin 1x removed
Harry David Mildenhall (1892 -)
Grandfather of DNA Match
William Mildenhall (1851 - 1908)
Father of Harry David Mildenhall
James Mildenhall (1821 -)
Father of William Mildenhall
George Mildenhall (1795 - 1875)
Father of James Mildenhall
Jonathan Mildenhall (1764 -)
Father of George Mildenhall
Susan Mildenhall (1797 - 1846)
Daughter of Jonathan Mildenhall
Sarah Martin (1830 - 1916)
Daughter of Susan Mildenhall

Predicted relationship: Distant Cousins
Possible range: 5th - 8th cousins
Confidence: Moderate
7cm 1 segment

DNA Match
5th cousin
Robert Karl Foster Snr (1932 -)
Grandfather of DNA Match
Ernest Frank Foster (1908 - 1986)
Father of Robert Karl Foster Snr
Grace Wadey (1881 - 1946)
Mother of Ernest Frank Foster
George Wadey (1845 -)

Father of Grace Wadey
Job Wadey (1780 -)
Father of George Wadey
Harriet Wadey (1828 - 1921)
Daughter of Job Wadey
Emma Ruth Pelling (1864 - 1932)
Daughter of Harriet Wadey

Brown
232. posted 14 Apr 2019, 14:25

Back to the Mustart descendants. Found a brothers marrying sisters again and though quite common, writing it up.

Robert Laing married Catherine McLaren in 1897, presumably in Ayrshire. They had two boys and then moved to England where they had at least a couple more children.

Richard Brown married Mary Jane Fisher on the 27th September 1893 in Wiltshire. They had 5 children, 1 of which died. Edith & Ivy were 2 of the survivors.

Alexander Laing married Edith Annie Brown in Eton in 1927. His younger brother Robert Paterson Mclaren Laing, married Ivy Catherine Elizabeth Brown a year later, also in Eton.

Alexander Paterson Laings
233. posted 15 Apr 2019, 08:33

I think I might have had the wrong Alexander Paterson Laing as a civil engineer in the 'Achievers' post. I have 3 of them now and I am not sure which one did what when.

It doesn't help that there aren't any death docs or 1911 census docs for Scotland. I guess they might be on ScotlandsPeople but not paying for that.

1. Alexander Paterson Laing born 20th July 1866 in Stirling. He appears to be working as a telegraph messenger at the age of 15. He then left for South Africa on the Norman on the 24th October 1896. On the 6th March 1923 he is living at 49 Catherine Ave, Johannesburg according to the UK civil engineers list. I have a doc indicating that he died in Cape Town in 1932 but public trees have him dying in Scotland on the 6th January 1932. The probate docs also confirm death as being at Langley House, Liberton, Edinburgh on this date. The executor of his will was his wife Augusta Harrison and it was valued at £229 17s 6d.

2. Alexander Paterson Laing was born on the 3rd September 1895 in Maritzburg, South Africa, the son of Alexander Paterson Laing and Augusta Harrison. On the 15th November 1920 he is listed as a civil engineer at Langley House but maybe this was his father? However, travel documents seem to confirm that he was a civil engineer like his father. He went from Durban to Southampton on the Edinburgh Castle in May 1938, his occupation is given as civil engineer.

He went from Durban to Southampton after his father had died on the Athlone Castle in April 1950. This time occupation given as engineer. Public trees have him marrying a Phyllis in South Africa but don't have a death date.

3. Alexander Paterson Laing was born c1888 in Logie. I think he was in the Navy, possibly as a reserve. In 1918 he is in Partick and his occupation is given as Naval Architect. Public trees have him marrying Margaret Hutton Napier in 1916 and dying in Ayr in 1945. This was the one I thought was the civil engineer that I now think is either 1 or 2. Still, Naval Architect sounds better!

Robt Chas Paterson
234. posted 15 Apr 2019, 09:06

A Mary Elizabeth Laing McLean was born in Learmonth, Victoria in 1868. Her parents are given as Mary Paterson and Andrew McLean. The only Mary Paterson it could be (from what I have in tree at present) is not descendant from Laing so I am not convinced I have the correct one. The Mary Paterson I have tentatively connected this husband and daughter to is the daughter of Charles Paterson and Jean Mustart. The Mary that is the mother dies in

Victoria in 1909 and the death doc gives the parents as Robt Chas Paterson and Mustard.

So many questions!! Is Charles Paterson really called Robert Charles Paterson? Why would Mary and Andrew give Laing as a middle name? Well that is only 2 but I really don't know if this is what happened to Mary.

Captain
235. posted 15 Apr 2019, 12:05

Allan Paterson Cousin was born in Clifton, Queensland on the 29th March 1900, son of John McLean Cousin and Jane McLean. (Haven't established a link if any yet - though Cousin comes up as a middle name somewhere else too as well as the McLean coincidence)

On the 1st May 1929 in Sydney, Allan was engaged as a 2nd mate on the RMMS Aorangi. His race is given as English rather than Scottish or Australian. The Aorangi sailed fromVancover, arriving in Honolulu on the 5th June 1929. He was still a 2nd mate in 1933 when he is on the Hauraki sailing from British Columbia and arriving in California on the 9th December 1933.
In 1933 he is listed on the UK Naval lists as a Lieutenant Commander of the seagoing Royal Australian Naval Reserve. (There are lots of other entries on these lists that I haven't looked at because there is so much info on the web about him and from the transcription below he was in the Royal Australian Navy from 1913 for 10 years before being in the merchant navy for 17 years and hence a reserve.) According to the transcription he served in WW2 and there is more info on him on the tinterweb including that he received the Distinguished Service Order for his service inWW2 which appears to be mainly on H.M.A.S. Katoomba:-

http://adb.anu.edu.au/biography/cousin-allan-paterson-9843

https://www.awm.gov.au/collection/R1513418/

https://discoveringanzacs.naa.gov.au/browse/records/472436

http://www.navy.gov.au/hmas-katoomba

204

In 1938 he is on the New Zealand electoral rolls as a mariner on SS Kaponga. By 1958 he is back in Australia, occupation Master Mariner living at 12 Overend St, Norman Park, Griffith, Bulimba. Also at this address is a Glena Thelma Cousin who I assumed was his wife but the biography doesn't mention her.

According to his biography (link above) on 22 December 1949 at Mowbraytown Presbyterian Church, East Brisbane, he married a divorcee Cena Ethel Gundry, née Christesen (d.1974) and he died in 1976. Here is a little bit about him from Who's Who in Australia, 1921-1950:-

"*COUSIN, Capt. Alan Paterson, R.D.,D.S.O., R.A.N.R. (S): son of John Cousin, Dollar, Scotland; b Mar. 29 1900, Clifton, Qld. ed. State Schools Toowoomba, Qld and R.A.N. Coll. Geelong and Jervis Bay; R.A.N. 1913-1923, then R.A.N.R. (S); 17 years in Union S.S. Co. ships, mobilised 1941, Commdr; C.O. H.M.A.S Manoora and Sen. Nav. Officer Aust. Landing Ships 1944-7 (Capt. 1945), took part in assault landings at Tannamerah Bay (Hollandia), Wadke I., Morotai, Panoan (Leyte I.). Lingayen, Tarakan, Labuan, and Balik Papan; Commanded H.M.A.S. Kanimbla 1948 until ship paid off in Syd. Mar 1949; demobilised 1949; club, United Service (Brisb.); address Overend St, Norman Park,Brisb.*"

Dull
236. posted 15 Apr 2019, 20:47

I have, apart from an hour to watch episode 1 of season 8 of GoT, been doing ancestry all day. 8 hours of looking at the Mustart distant cousins. I haven't done an all dayer in ages. It's been quite nice to have loads of new cousins to review. However nothing of much interest to report as they all seem to go to Canada or I lose track of them. I'm only mentioning the following 2 as I feel I need to write something after all that work!

First is not even blood. William Kilpatrick is the stepson of Mary Anne Wotherspoon. He was born in 1862 in Ardrossan. When he was 19, he was in lodgings in Glasgow and he is an arts student. Did he go to the Glasgow School of Arts? It was established in 1845 so it was there in 1881, although the Mackintosh Building wasn't built then. William did not have a career in art, by 1891 he has moved to Edinburgh and is the minister of Gorgie Free

Church. He marries Mary and they have at least a couple of children. In 1901 he is Minister Of W F Church.

Next is John Wotherspoon. John was born c1893 in Shettleston, Lanarkshire, son of John Wotherspoon and Margaret Campbell. By 1911, aged 18. he had moved to Devon and was working as a marine engineer. No idea what happened to him after that.

Truly dull if they are the best two stories of the day! Though the son of a plumber going to art school inVictorian times is pretty cool and I'm sure I have not seen an arts student before.

Notre Dame
237. posted 16 Apr 2019, 12:50

Half of it burnt down yesterday. I was only there just over a month ago.

Theory
238. posted 16 Apr 2019, 23:04

What we know:-

1. Charles Paterson married Jean Mustart in Stirling on the 14th December 1818.
2. Charles and Jean appear with 4 daughters in the 1841 census.
3. According to public trees Charles dies in 1845.
4. Elizabeth marries in 1851 and emigrates to New York.
5. Mary is a servant in 1851. She marries in 1860 and emigrates to Australia.
6. Rachel is also a servant in 1851 (only 13!). She marries in 1857 and stays in Stirling.
7. In 1861, Jean is living with her daughter Rachel and her family.
8. According to public trees, Jean dies in 1869.

9. My children and nephew can link to Jean through their DNA match. This means that Alexander is their son, bringing known children to 5.

Annoyances:-
Why do none of their children have baptism docs? (Been annoying me for 7+ years, always will)
Why do none of their children have middle names? The Scottish thing of having other grandparent surnames as middle names is really helpful!

Questions:-
What happened to Janet? Janet Paterson is too common a name, impossible.
Where was Jean in 1851? We know she was alive in 1861.
Charles and Jean married in 1818 - surely they had children before Alexander in 1825?

Theory:-

There is an 1851 census for a Jean Paternos 55 Hellen Paternos 29 Janet Paternos 20. This would place Jean and Janet in 1851, it's obviously just a typo but I can't view Scottish docs. However - who is Hellen? She wasn't on the 1841 census. In 1841, Hellen is living with her older brother James. These two extra children, c1817 and c1822 help to fill in the missing childbirth years. What throws a spanner in the works though, is also on this 1851 census are grandchildren: Jean Stepherson 8, Elizabeth Stepherson 5, Hellen Stepherson 2 and I currently have no idea who they are. I am currently working on a theory that Charles and Jean had at least 8 children rather than the known about 5.

SS Lesbian
239. posted 17 Apr 2019, 20:52

James Wylie was born in Kincardine, Perthshire on the 17th April 1822. He started a seamanship apprenticeship c1838. James married Christian Dunn on the 18th November 1849 and they went on to have at least 6 children. James does not appear on any census docs until he has retired so it can be assumed he was at sea most of the time. Christian and their children lived with her mother, Janet Mustart in 1851 and 1861. However Christian must have travelled sometimes with her husband as their daughter Mary was born at sea in 1863.

James finished his apprenticeship on the 11th March 1851. He became a Master Mariner on the 28th September 1855.

Public trees have James as dying on the 19th July 1895 at 24 North Fort St. North Leith, Edinburgh.

There is a document that might be him which gives a death of the 20th August 1895. This says he was on the *SS Lesbian* working as a fireman in the Bay of Biscay when he drowned. As he would have been 73, I don't think this is him.

Another Rev
240. posted 18 Apr 2019, 10:12

Robert Wylie was born in North Leith on the 30th July 1851 and was baptised on the 3rd August. On the 31st July 1865 he began an apprenticeship to his father, James Wylie, on the ship SS Ormelie. The apprenticeship was only for 4 years.
Robert is not located in 1871 or 1881. However, in 1884 he married Stewart Borwick in Edinburgh. Robert and Stewart had at least 3 children before moving to North London. They had at least 2 more children in London. In 1891, Robert is a Presbyterian Minister. Robert and all of his family emigrated to New Zealand in 1897, sailing on the Tongariro.

Steward died in Auckland on the 18th March 1920 and Robert died there a couple of years later on the 20th July 1923. What was he doing for the 20 years he is not located? Presumably becoming a Reverend but quite a change from working on his fathers ship.

A quick mention of David Wylie Henderson. David was born in North Leith on the 29th November 1881. In 1901 he is living with his Aunt and he is an arts student. Was very surprised to see a second arts student so soon after finding the first one. No idea what happens to him.

Bloomers
241. posted 18 Apr 2019, 19:51

Alfred Mustart was born in Dagenham on the 6th November 1904. Alfred emigrated to Australia on the 9th May 1922, on the Largs Bay. Sometime between his arrival and 1929, he married Helen Margaret Martha Thompson in South Australia.

On the 23rd March 1929, Alfred was found guilty of *"...for the unlawful possession of two pairs of bloomers, string of pearls, kimona, etc. at Mount Gambier..."* He was fined £10 and costs of 15s which he paid.

Alfred went back to England a couple of times. He arrived at Southampton on the 5th June 1933 and the 22nd September 1953. Alfred had 5 short stints working on the Western Australian Railways but always left of his own accord. 7-19th Dec 1962, a Repairer at Geraldton. 7-17th Feb 1966, a T/Goods Porter at Perth Goods. 17th June - 15th August 1966, a Repairer at Wurarga. 7th April - 5th May 1967, a T Repairer at Yargoo and finally 29th-31st July 1968, a labourer at workshop.

Alfred died in Perth in 1973.

Book 5
242. posted 18 Apr 2019, 20:23

I think I have done the Alexander Mustart & Christian Paton descendants as much as I can now. Seems like a logical place to stop and make a start on the next *'Ramblings...'* book. Think it's under a year since last one so not sure if there will be enough entries to warrant it. I don't think I want it called *'Ramblings...'*

INDEX

John Green 88, 176
Stephen Green 87, 125, 126, 157
William Green 125
John Hoad 185
Thomas Hoad 155
Nicholas Hubbard 184
William Malthouse 79
Edward Manser 222
Ward Meadows 167
George Pell 152, 181
Robert Pell 23
John Nicholls 184
Thomas Sayer Nicholls 106
William Scotney 156
John Shelley 135
William Shelley 187
Edward Stapleton 180
Timothy Suter 166, 181, 183
Frederick Taylor 157
John Wilson 173, 181
Sarah Wilson 172

MADDOX

Joseph Custerson 76
John William Maddox 230
Jonathan Mildenhall 231
Richard Martin 104
Robert Pelling 230
John Stafford 110
Henry Stone 61
Job Wadey 231

Michael Minter 66
John Nelms 67
Margaret Reeve 60
William Relfe 60
William Shaw 62
Mary Wilson 65
Steven Yearsley 67

GREEN

Benjamin Clapson 9
Goddard Cruttenden 169
John Cruttenden 36
Henry Cruttenden 36
William Cruttenden 169
Mary Gascain 9
Thomas Manser 9
Richard Pettifer 84
Sarah Ann Piper 15
John Shelley 138

STORIES

BRAIN

Valentine Bowles 66
Arnold Costin 123
Crowhurst 130
Mary Hollands 72
Kenardington 68
Limpsfield 130
Marden 60
William Relfe 63
Ruardean 67

MADDOX

PATERSON

DNA EXTRAS

BUS STOP
Green Park
Station
9
14
38

TO
BREXIT

Hey Cocksplats
If it smells like   and
it looks like   and it
sounds like   , then it
Must be
BREXSHIT
THIS IS BIGGER THAN YOUR EGO –
WAKE UP AND SEE THE DAMAGE
THAT YOU ARE RESPONSIBLE FOR !
AND THEY'RE STILL CONNING YOU